Anxiety

How to Overcome Jealousy, negative Thinking and Insecirity, learn how to Eliminate Conflicts and more ...

By Robert Miller

Table of content:

Introduction 5

Chapter 1: Understanding Couples therapy 7

1.1 What is Couples therapy? 7

1.2 How does Couple therapy work? 13

1.3 Couple therapy as a beneficial source to reconnect 21

Chapter 2: A Theory of Change 24

2.1 Conceptions of Human Personality 24

2.2 Wanted: A wise and humble Counselor 25

2.3 A fully Sensible, Tested, and Effective Approach to Helping Couples 29

2.4 Therapy a Positive Growth Experience for Couples 34

2.5 Addressing the Couple's Context 39

Chapter 3: Specific Problematic Areas for Couples 45

3.1 Chronic or Unproductive Arguments 45

3.2 Verbal Abuse 55

3.3 Separating work from Home Life 62

3.4 Sexual issues and Problems 65

Chapter 4: The Georama; a Window into the Psyche 80

4.1 Johari's window into Psyche 80

4.2   How to observe someone's Psyche? 85

4.3 Relaxing Couples by Assigning Activities (or you can do by self-help)..........103

4.4 Music therapy Activities and Tools 108

4.5 Art therapy Techniques for De-stressing........................123

Chapter 5: Deepening Connections and Bonds...............132

5.1 Emotional Connection...132

5.2 Relationship Therapy: Enhancing Romantic Relationships............................136

Chapter 6: Psychodynamic Upgrades 164

6.1 Focusing on Hidden Issues, Fears, and Desires................167

6.2 Focusing on Transference: 195

6.3 Focusing on Projective Identification 200

6.4 Focusing on Acceptance and Forgiveness.....................206

Conclusion 217

References 219

Introduction

Each and every relationship has its very own ups and downs, but how a couple tackle that tough time in their relationship is all that matters and has an impact on the longevity of the bond. Anxiety, negativity, and jealousy are just like the enemies of relationships. It is impossible for a person to not feel jealousy, anxiety, and negativity while being in a relationship. This book will help the couple to identify, overcome, and avoid the situations that are damaging to the relationship. You should have control over these aspects in a relationship for the relationship to endure for a lifetime companionship. When a person is in a relationship, other things that should be considered are compromise, self-evaluation, and forgiveness. For a relationship to be successful, it is required that both the individuals are honest with each other about every aspect of their life. One should not be lying to his or her partner just for the sake of them for not hurting them. It's better to be honest, and face the situation and outcomes rather than the person finding out the truth from someone else. Self-confidence and self-esteem for one's own self are also a guarantee of a healthy relationship. Fun activities, planned dates, outing, and vacations with your partner are an integral part of having a happy and healthy relationship. Both individuals should have the liberty and independence to do whatever they want for their career as well as other activities outside the relationship. Continuously nagging each other every single day can tear off the bond and spark between the couple, eventually leading towards the death of the relationship.

Chapter 1: Understanding Couples therapy

This chapter explains an understanding of Couples therapy in all perspectives. You can also get the idea that how couples therapy work in the favor of couples. How couple therapy works as a beneficial source to reconnect couples and the whole phenomena behind it, all aspects are discussed in detail in a given chapter below.

1.1 What is Couples therapy?

Counseling is for people who are married or are committed to each other. This is also referred to as a therapy for family. The purpose of couple therapy is to enhance and improve the relationship status of the couples. That form of counseling also help couples determine whether they should stay together or not. There are occasions when one or both parties need to discuss the psychological problems individually.

Understanding:

Therapy also involves sessions aimed at enhancing problem-solving, developing communication skills, and defining life goals and expectations for relationships. Many common problems include infidelity, financial difficulties, illness, and other changes in life, as well as frustration.

Counseling can be short-term or over a period of several months, depending on the extent of difficulties in relationship. If you and your wife are having problems because you end up in a big dispute any time you disagree, and fix absolutely nothing. The two of you are slowly growing apart due to the intense tension in the relationship. You have always thought about leaving your partner, but first, you want to try a couple therapy.

You are in counseling, and you understand that you both need guidance with the way you interact, and with your approach to problem-solving techniques. You also discover that you are simply continuing a form of behavior that was demonstrated by your parents: they yelled and accomplished nothing, and eventually fell apart and divorced. You can now change your actions with your newly gained awareness that part of the issue is that you follow what you have seen your parents do. You strengthen the relationship over time using constructive communication strategies and a workable issue solution. Positive feelings resurface for your partner, and you won't be able to believe that you had wanted to break the relationship.

Five Principles of Effective Couples therapy:

5 basic principles of effective couple's therapy are as follows:

1. Changes the views of the relationship:

Throughout the counseling process, the therapist tries to help both parties take a more realistic view of the relationship. They learn to avoid the "blame game" and look more at what happens to them in a cycle that includes both partners. You may also benefit from ensuring that their relationship exists in a specific context. For instance, couples who struggle financially may be put under different forms of situational stress than those who do not. Therapists begin this process by gathering "evidence" about the partners 'relationship by observing how they communicate. Therapists then formulate

"hypotheses" about what factors could contribute to the problems in their relationship between the partners. Therapists share the knowledge with the couple according to the basic psychological perspective of the therapist and it also varies from couple to couple. With a range of methods, from clinical to insight-oriented, there is empirical support. Different therapists can use various approaches, but as long as they work on improving the perception of the relationship, the couple will begin to see each other and their experiences in a more constructive way.

2. Modifies dysfunctional behavior:

Good couple therapists try to improve the way the partners actually communicate with one another. In addition to helping them enhance their relationship, this means that therapists do need to ensure that their clients do not participate in behaviors that can cause physical, psychological, or economic damage.

To do so, therapists must carry out a detailed evaluation to decide if their clients are genuinely at risk. For example, if possible, the therapist may recommend that one person be sent to a shelter for domestic violence, a specialist clinic for substance abuse, or anger management. It is also likely that if the risk isn't serious enough, the couple can benefit from "time-out" measures to avoid conflict escalation.

3. Decreases emotional avoidance:

Couples that refrain from sharing their private feelings are at greater risk of being emotionally isolated and growing apart. Efficient couple therapists help their clients put out the feelings and ideas they are unable to convey to others. Couple counseling based on intimacy helps couples to feel less anxious to communicate their desire for closeness. According to this view, some partners in childhood who have failed to build "free" emotional attachments have unmet needs that they bring into their adult relationships. They are afraid to show their partners how much they need them because they are afraid their partners are going to reject them. Behavioral therapists believe that adults may be unable to communicate their true feelings because they have not received "reinforcement" in the past. Either way, all psychological strategies recommend encouraging their clients to convey their true feelings in a way that would ultimately bring them back together.

4. Improves communication:

Intimacy is one of the "three C's" of being able to communicate. All positive couple therapies are geared towards helping the couples connect more effectively. Building on concepts 2 and 3, this contact should not be violent, nor will partners make one another crazy as they share their true feelings. Therefore, couples can need "coaching" in order to learn to talk to one another in a more supportive and understanding way. The therapist can also give instructional advice to the couple and provide them with the basis for understanding what forms of communication are successful and what forms would only create more tension. For example, they could learn how to listen more actively and empathetically. Just how to achieve this step, however, allows therapists to switch back to the tests they carried out early in care. Couples with a persistent history of mutual criticism can involve an approach different from those who seek to avoid confrontation at all costs.

5. Promote strengths:

Good couple therapists point out the strengths of the relationship and develop resilience, particularly when therapy is about to end. Since so much couple counseling includes concentrating on problem areas, it's easy to lose sight of the other areas where couple work effectively. Promoting strength is about helping the couple gain more satisfaction from their relationship. The behaviorally focused therapist can "prescribe" one partner to do something agreeable to another. Perhaps therapists from other orientations who concentrate more on feelings may help the couple create a more optimistic "plot" or narrative about their relationship. In this case, the therapist should stop trying to put his or her own perspective on what constitutes a strength and let the couple determine this.

We can see, then, that if their life seems hopeless, people in strained relationships need not give up in despair. In the same way, people who are reluctant to enter into long-term relationships will be motivated to learn how to repair problem relationships.

Looking at the other side, these five concepts of good counseling recommend strategies for partners to develop healthy close relationships and sustain them. Take an unbiased look at your relationship, seek assistance in eliminating unhealthy habits, feel like you can express your feelings, connect openly, and show what works. Most importantly, by ensuring that each partnership has its own specific challenges and strengths, you can give yours the best survival chances.

1.2 How does Couple therapy work?

Counseling will benefit couples with the use of the above approaches and more. For couple counseling to succeed, both people must be committed to enhancing their partnership while looking inwardly at their own strengths and weaknesses. Knowing their behaviors and habits that make your partner tick could have a positive impact on making improvements in both personal aspect and relationships. Couple's therapy is not intended to unload anger, frustration, and other negative actions against

13

one spouse. It's about finding passion, commitment, and all the other approaches that lead a healthy relationship.

Does Marriage Counseling Work? That's a very big issue, but what people are really talking about is, "Will marriage therapy save my marriage? The response to that is very much based on a variety of variables beyond the counselor's office.

Although some of these points are highlighted below, some of the considerations to look for when seeking marital therapy are as follows:

1.   Did you just wait too long? If you have been breaking each other apart for ten years, there is a very good risk that there is so much harm that it cannot be done to undo.

2.   Need to save your marriage, really? People often go to therapy just to claim they've tried. They just don't want it to work. They save face just to assuage their remorse.

3.   Is there harassment or aggression in the relationship? If there is a family, you're not trying to save it; you're trying to avoid the illegal activity. Abusers, whether physical or mental, are not "unhappy" in their marriage; they are often terrified

and impotent people who feel helpless in their lives anywhere else.

4.   Will the structure meet your needs? If saving your marriage means spending another 30 years doing away with everything you want to do, is that worth it? It takes a hard and truthful look at what every person needs to make sure you get exactly that what you need out of the relationship.

One of the most important factors in relationship counseling's success is the counselor. Nearly every counselor in the world claims they're doing marital therapy, but most never received any preparation. They also have a psychology or counseling degree and believe they should do it.

Marriage therapy is not about one person and their problems. There are two individuals, their problems and the relationship and dynamics of these things.

Marriage therapy is not just therapy – it's an advanced talent that requires a specialist.

1)   Statistics Show High Rates of Patient Satisfaction:

There are high rates of patient satisfaction demonstrated by families and couples who attended family or couple counseling sessions. Over 98 percent of the surveys reported having received good or excellent couple counseling, and more than 97 percent said they had the support they wanted. 93 percent of clients, having met with a marriage or family therapist, said they had more powerful resources to cope with their problems. Respondents have indicated improved physical health after completing therapy and the ability to perform better at work.

2) Marriage or Family Counseling consumes Less Time than Individual Counseling:

If you ask yourself, "does marriage therapy work?" The response can depend on whether your partner is willing or not to go with you to therapy. When your partner refuses to go with you to therapy, you will change the dynamics of your relationship only by going to individual counseling. Statistics, however, indicate that couples or family therapy are typically faster and more effective than single therapy alone. If a couple or a family goes together to counseling, they have the ability to focus on the dynamics of their community, and this leads them to more rapid results. Usually, reaching a target in family or couple therapy takes about one third fewer sessions than it does in individual therapy. This means you're going to spend less money and get your marriage back on track faster than if you're only trying to help out.

3)   Emotionally Focused Therapy Works:

Here exists no magical cure that can repair a broken relationship, but many therapists have had great success using the Emotionally Focused Therapy or EFT method of therapy. When asked, "does therapy work in marriage?" Statistics show that when couples use EFT, the answer is usually yes. EFT works by helping a person understand their emotional reactions to events and reorganize them. Working with their emotional cycles will give a couple a deeper understanding of each other, and this can help them build new relationship cycles. Ninety percent of them record major changes in their partnership when couples turn to EFT. Between 70 and 75 percent of depressed couples will switch to recovery using EFT. EFT basically lets a couple foster their relationship in a safe and successful manner.

4)   Couples Therapy Works Better When Couples Seek for Help Early:

Sadly, there are no clear statistics to support this claim, but therapists usually assume the answer to "does marriage therapy work? "And most often when the couple seeks counseling at the earliest possible moment. When a couple waits until their issues are too far advanced, one person might already have given up on the relationship, and it may be difficult to save the relationship at that stage. For other situations, contact habits have been so aggressive or hostile that the therapist may be unable to teach the couple new strategies for contact. The couples will pursue counseling as soon as possible for the best chance of success. Even couples may wish to sign up for premarital counseling.

5) Degrees May Not Matter much; The Importance of Finding a Therapist Who Is Right for You:

Statistics shows that it does not matter how much knowledge the marriage therapist has. A poll of 4,000 respondents found that irrespective of whether they saw a psychologist, therapist, or social worker, people feel the same about their therapy.

Researchers felt the treatment was less successful in situations where patients only had a small range of options because of limitations imposed by their insurance provider. Since the effectiveness levels of various mental health providers seem to vary very little, you may simply want to select your therapist based on your intuition. If it sounds like you could be assisted by a specific therapist, then schedule a session. If not, then speak to another expert.

6) Marriage Counseling Requires Shopping Around:

Surveys show that in private practice, about eighty percent of therapists do pair therapy. How they got their training is a mystery because most therapists working today have never taken a few counseling courses and have never done their internships under the guidance of someone who perfected the craft. In the point of view of a person going in for couple therapy is like getting your broken leg fixed by a doctor who missed orthopedics in medical school. It's important not to just pick someone nearby or even someone who has a degree, to look for someone who has been qualified in marriage counseling. Ask them, look up their qualifications online, and ask for feedback from other therapists. Has marriage therapy ever been fully educated in marital counseling with the person doing the counseling? Not much and not very often.

7) The pain of Breakup Needs to Outweigh the Pain of Marriage

Change happens when the pain of remaining the same is greater than the pain of change. It may sound like a strange assertion, but it's real. Most of us don't find divorce less difficult than remaining together; however, it can be. There are few factors that can cause pain in a marriage. Consider if breaking up is not what's best for you, the family, and the other person when contemplating therapy (and that can be the number one conversation with a great counselor).

One wants to believe it, but there are moments when it was a mistake to get married, and it is something you can reverse. If you've built a life, though, started a family and shared years together, that's a decision that needs to be taken with sensitivity.

If your marriage has ended or is on the rocks and you know a couple who have recently married or are considering it, persuade them to get therapy now. They shouldn't wait for their marriage to fall apart. Much as you go to a doctor every year, constantly focusing on it will look to keep your marriage safe. Was marital therapy successful in this case? Yes. Especially when it comes to getting it when you need it the most.

1.3 Couple therapy as a beneficial source to reconnect

Couple counseling will benefit couples with the use of the above approaches and more. For couple counseling to succeed, all parties need to be committed to strengthening their relationship while looking inwardly at their own strengths and weaknesses. Knowing their behaviors and habits that make your partner tick could have a positive impact on making improvements in both personal and partnerships aspect. Couple counseling is not intended to unload anger, frustration, and other negative habits to one spouse. It's about finding passion, commitment, and all the other approaches that go into a good relationship.

Couple's therapist looks into the ins and outs of the relationship between the couple and gives them insight into their mutual strengths and weaknesses as well as their personalities. The therapist serves as a neutral mediator and gives all partners advice. He or she can encourage more two-way contact, build more constructive ways of communicating and thinking, and multiple ways the couple can show each other their affection and support while in the therapy process.

Couple therapy, in any case, does not benefit everyone; many people still express their concern for couple therapy and methods of reconnecting with their spouse. Many of the advantages of combination therapy include:

High Levels of Satisfaction:

Couples show higher levels of satisfaction and overall happiness during counseling sessions and then afterward. Ninety-seven percent of couples surveys said they got the support they wanted. They said they were given the tools their therapist needed to make more rational decisions about their relationships. The overall mental and physical health, as well as job results, improved as a side effect.

It Doesn't Take Much Time:

Normally, a couple therapist has seen and heard all of it, from the smallest issues to the most serious relationship problems. If couples are having joint meetings, it can take a few meetings to address the issues, because therapists have various approaches and strategies. This could take more time to try and fix issues yourself, and seeing a licensed professional would save you both time and energy.

You'll Know the Answers:

Occasionally, counseling will convince you that you really are meant to be with your partner. Sometimes, it could demonstrate that your relationship isn't what any of you wants, which sometimes leads to divorce and separation. Regardless, couple counseling leads to questions answered, fewer "what-ifs" and more satisfaction.

Chapter 2: A Theory of Change

In this chapter, the concept of a theory of change is given in detail. What is a wise and humble counselor and how he works, how to access a sensible, tested and an effective approach for helping partners in any commitment by understanding their root issues, these all aspects are discussed in depth and detail. How to make a therapy as a positive growth experience for couples and actual ways of addressing the couple's context are also mentioned in this chapter.

2.1 Conceptions of Human Personality

There are three distinct conceptions of the human personality, that is, the autonomous, the verbal, and the social entity. All of these means different relations between the person and the group and different causality theories.

Change in a person is a logical reordering of human thought processes from the autonomous individual perspective. The cause of any personal improvement is a reasonable individual effort. That viewpoint is expressed in clinical psychology and psychoanalysis. A growing person has an inner desire to selfactualize from the articulate perspective, which is the cause of change.

That view is based on humanistic psychology. The person is a cultural being from the perspective of social individuals, necessarily dependent on others, who grow a mind only in contact with others. From this viewpoint, it is difficult to distinguish individual change from a change in the groups to which an individual belongs.

Some defined the cycle of transition as the mechanisms of change reflect a mid-level distinction between a full psychotherapy framework and the theory of the techniques proposes. This description appears to describe more of what was called the treatment process.

2.2 Wanted: A wise and humble Counselor

The best counselors in the profession are not always those who are well known, but instead, those who still achieve perfection and flat out to work harder than anyone else. These counselors are actively asking what they are doing and why, being brutally frank about their research and its outcomes. They also receive input from their clients and friends, asking for the most honest evaluations of what works and what doesn't. Most of all, they are always so modest that they don't seek recognition or the limelight but go about their remarkable dedication to helping others in a peaceful way.

What, overall, makes a great counselor?

A truly great counselor combines all facets of successful therapy through masterfully establishing a relational relationship, instilling optimism, rapidly concentrating on realistic objectives, choosing evidence-based interventions wisely, optimizing incentives for out-of-session on improvement, and encouraging commitment and follow-up to care to ensure that recovery results are sustained long after termination.

A successful counselor is also an individual who is completely dedicated to the clients or students they represent. We know that professionally and socially, we have to be engaged in continuous development to become the best resource. They have the opportunity to see beyond the spoken word and understand what is really happening in the life of a client or student in even the unheard words. A great counselor is someone who loves helping those they represent to get motivated by encouraging their clients and students to become problem-solvers for their lives. Finally, a great counselor works out of a position with a client by helping [that person] learn how to handle life by themselves through some daily mental health check-ups.

Great counselors also have a passion for supporting others. We have respect for those we support, and they understand their positions in the therapy process. Good counselors are always committed to the practice of therapy and recognize the value of professional unity. Concomitantly, excellent experts understand each other. We know their core values and beliefs and foresee precisely how their core values and beliefs impact the therapy process. Superior counselors always have fun and use goodnatured and kind humor. Finally, excellent counselors show a degree of tenacity that fosters sustained client engagement — even when the therapy process is challenging.

Most useful skills to possess as a counselor:
Highly valued is an ability to genuinely listen to the spoken and unspoken and an ability to build partnerships with a diverse clientele.

Any other valuable skills or qualities that a counselor should possess are as follows:

a) Self-awareness — self-awareness, including behaviors, beliefs, and emotions, and the ability to consider how and what factors can affect you as a counselor

b)   Empathy and comprehension — the ability to put yourself in another's position, even if that person is totally different from you

c)   Versatility — the ability to do so as a counselor to meet clients' needs so that a counselor can establish and maintain a therapeutic relationship and clients' benefit.

More than ten keys to being a better counselor:

1. Knowing what really works in therapy research.

2. Understanding what counseling is.

3. Knowing how to intervene adequately.

4. Capable of using the body as an instrument (the key weapon in the arsenal of the counselor).

5. Comprising your own emotions.

6. Understand the main value of mourning and properly doing so.

7. Proper self-disclosure (it's not about you, really).

8. Silence used and tolerated (especially for those who prefer extraversion).

9. Understand breathing's role in therapy.

10. Trusting and feeling respect for yourself.

The most overrated and underrated skill to have as a counselor:

Relationship building skills are significant, but Freud has identified much of the link that leads to a successful marital relationship as transference. It is one of the toughest things new counselors can endure, the conundrum of why couldn't they communicate with that client. Often the question of communicating has more to do with features (e.g., "You remind me of ...") than any ability or actions.

Experience is what you receive when you unsuccessfully try something. Good advisors have much experience.

2.3 A fully Sensible, Tested, and Effective Approach to Helping Couples

The effectiveness of marital therapy is directly linked to the level of motivation and timing of both partners. Marriage therapy is actually divorced therapy for certain couples, as they have already thrown in the towel. For example, one or both partners may already have agreed to end the marriage, and he/she uses therapy as a way to disclose it to their spouse. The issues in a marriage can often be too deep and long-standing to be successful in therapy. For others, they aren't genuinely expressing their problems with the therapist.

Furthermore, finding a therapist who has experience working with couples and is a good match for both you and your partner is important. When the therapist may not feel secure with both participants, this can have a negative effect on progress; or one participant can drop out prematurely.

Timing is an important factor in the workings of marital therapy. Unfortunately, most couples are waiting too long to reach out for assistance in fixing their marriage. Couples are waiting an average of six years of unhappiness before seeking support, according to some research. Think for a few minutes about the figure. Couples have six years to build up frustration before they start the essential work of learning to effectively overcome differences.

For starters as an example, Rachel and Jeff sat down on the sofa and started discussing their longtime feud over how to handle money and whether or not Rachel could go back to college and graduate from an education so she could change jobs. They have the same dispute with no resolution over and over again, tell by Rachel, she has been working in an insurance business for ten years and hate her job, but Jeff is blocking her attempts to join a profession that would make her happier.

When it's Jeff's turn to offer his opinion on things, he says: They just bought a house and have two young kids. For Rachel, this is actually not a good time to get a degree. He helped her get through her undergraduate degree in her mid-twenties when they were first married, and she doesn't even know if she's going to enjoy becoming a teacher.

So the first step to helping Rachel and Jeff strengthen their relationship is to allow them to come to terms with identifying the biggest issue in their relationship and for both of them to take their actions on their own so that they can do better. They need to have reasonable expectations, though, as negotiating can be a challenge when both partners have busy careers and kids.

It is important that partners see conflict as an unavoidable part of a romantic partnership dedicated to it. After all, there are ups and downs in any relationship, and conflict goes with the territory. But couples may avoid confrontation because it may have meant the end of the marriage of their parents or led to bitter controversies. In romantic relationships avoiding conflict backfires. Bottling up uneven thoughts and emotions doesn't allow the partner the ability to improve their behavior. One of the secrets of a successful marriage or romantic relationship is learning to carefully select fights and to differentiate between small and important problems.

Others describes "marital masters" as "people who are so good at coping with conflict that they make marital squabbles look enjoyable." A research showing significant disparities between couples whose relationships were successful and those heading for misery and/or divorce. It's not that some people aren't getting angry or disagreeing. That is why they are able to remain linked and communicate with each other when they disagree. They pepper their disagreements with displays of love, genuine curiosity, and mutual respect, rather than being aggressive and hurtful.

Seven tips to help deal with differences between you and your partner:

• Establishing a comfortable environment and frequently spending time with your partner so you can talk about your interests and goals.

• Don't give up on personal ambitions and stuff like hobbies or activities you want to do. This can only create frustration.

• Foster each other's passions. Agree you are not always expressing the same desires. Value the need for space for your companion if they want to go on holiday without you, etc.

• Learn how to skillfully manage disputes. Do not set aside resentments capable of ruining a partnership. Couples seeking to avoid conflict run the risk of forming dysfunctional relationships, which can put them at high risk of divorce.

• Facilitate an open dialogue. Listen to the questions of your companion, and ask for clarity on vague issues. Avoid threats, and do say things that you will later regret.

• Keep away from the "blame game." Take responsibility for your role in the issues and recognize that in some way, all human beings are flawed. The next time you're angry with your partner, find out what's happening inside you, and pause and reflect before you accuse them.

• Be honest about changing timescales. It takes more than a several sessions to shed light on the dynamics and initiate the change process.

How can marriage counseling help couples?

- Where dysfunctional relationship dynamics can be recognized early and decided upon, the actual change process will begin.

- With the resources offered by the therapist, an empowered couple may begin to discuss their issues from a different view and discover new ways of understanding and resolving disputes.

- Partners will start building trust and strengthening contact, which may have diminished the consistency of their interactions.

- A pair of counselors will provide "neutral ground" to help couples come to an understanding and work through difficult support issues.

- Couples may agree to restore their marriage and make a renewed commitment or explain the reasons for separating or terminating their marriage.

2.4 Therapy a Positive Growth Experience for Couples

The harsh truth is that maybe counseling won't improve. If a spouse has taken the divorce decision, it can be hard to undo. If the couple have been waiting too long to seek support, it may also be unsuccessful. Research shows couples wait an average of six years before they get support.

But the cycle will benefit those who didn't wait too long or those who commit to change. There are the following ways:

- If unhealthy relationship dynamics can be established early and accepted, the real change process will start.

- With the resources offered by the therapist, an empowered couple may begin to discuss their issues from a different view and discover new ways of understanding and resolving disputes.

- Partners will start building trust and strengthening contact, which may have diminished the consistency of their interactions.

- A counselor for couples will provide "neutral ground" to help couples come to terms and work through difficult support issues.

- Couples may agree to restore their marriage and make a renewed commitment or explain the reasons for separating or terminating the marriage.

Role of a Psychologist in Counseling:

Counseling psychologists help people with physical, social, and mental health problems, strengthen their sense of well-being, relieve feelings of distress, and overcome crises. This is the least requiring thing a person who seeks help can expect.

Preparation reflects an additional component in marriage and family Therapy (MFT). Supervision for at least a period of two years is by a certified clinician.

It normally takes two years to work at the Master level of counseling or marriage and family counseling. What state has separate licensing requirements, which usually involve an assessment?

The role of counselor or therapist is to:

- Observe experiences
- Evaluate and help fix issues
- Diagnose and treat conditions
- Navigate through difficult changes
- Recognize troubling patterns in relationships or behaviors
- Replace unhealthy behaviors with healthier ones.

How to find a great therapist:

While finding a therapist,

- Confirm that the therapist has the marital counseling qualifications and experience.

- Ask your psychiatrist about his/her opinion on divorce. Was the therapist geared towards remedies, or is she/he going to recommend that you get a divorce because the problem is difficult?

- Both you and your companion will be at ease with the therapist. The therapist will understand your perspective.

- Consider how Marriage is treated by your therapist. When the therapist is strict in describing what makes a successful marriage, then it is a red flag.

- Know that when you should give up your marriage, a therapist can't tell you exactly.

- Set deadlines early and make sure you make progress against them. If not, speak with the therapist about this.

- In order to move forward, it might be helpful to consider some of your previous experience, but if that is the priority, find a more forward-looking therapist.

How to Best Deal with Marriage Issues and Problems:

Research suggests that it is showing how couples describe each other's shortcomings. Researchers, for example, questioned newlyweds about the kinds of explanations they've used over a six-month span. The couples were also asked to identify and score stressful incidents outside their marriage.

The tests, performed for four years every six months, found the following:

- Low stress equaled more charitable explanations by spouses for each other's negative shortcomings

- High stress equaled an inability to offer charitable explanations, even though the individual did so during low-stress periods.

"Enduring flaws" has a lot to do with how we justify other people's behavior. Vulnerability encompasses cognitive types, personality characteristics, and experiences of childhood. These combine with different stressful experiences (work, worries about finances, health issues, etc.) and inform our explanations.

The Marriage Vulnerability-Stress- Adaptation-Model of Marriage (VSA) also explains how, over time, adaptive processes affect satisfaction.

When couples who think about the positive habits, their happiness is greater. Those that get trapped in the relationship's daily routine are less content.

But all the stress is negative, and it matters to our attitude around it. Managing or reducing it leads to improved health and wellness.

2.5 Addressing the Couple's Context

How Can We Restore a Marriage?

The response to that question is not easy. It's all up to how the marriage breaks down. For instance, if you've separated over time, then reconnecting is your priority.

Money and sex aren't the reasons couples fight according to his study. The underlying challenge is a lack of emotional correlation. Take charge and proceed as follows:

1. Consider relation challenger

2. Understand the maps of love for one another

3. Create a culture of respect and gratitude

What if your question is about infidelity? The trust has diminished. The first question is: can you trust your partner again? Would you believe you will contribute if trust is restored? Two more questions proposed are:

1. Have you let go of your anger and resentment over the abuse of your partner, and can you move forward?

2. Should you excuse your spouse for their actions?

If you can, then your partner needs to step up. For couples in this situation, the Confidence Revival Process has been created. In short, there are three stages to it: atone, attune, and add.

The cheater must prove trustworthy during expiation. This will probably take time throughout the course; he will not be able to blame the partner for what happened. The one who cheats must be held responsible without defensiveness for the affair. Honesty and full transparency is a must. The prerequisite is a statute called "no second chance." The cheater has to cut off all ties to the ex-lover.

Adding only occurs after pardon. The couple is ready to move on in this process, but they also need to know how to better handle conflicts. The cheater has to promise to make the relationship a priority. If you have kids, chances are they know what happened to some degree. Perhaps your in-laws and close friends know too.

During this process, the couple will declare their intention to commit to their marriage to those men. That allows the couple to be a source of help for those people.

Attachment requires the reconnection by physical contact with your partner. This has to happen to repair the relationship.

Issues are difficult to recover from; however, it does. Researcher recommends to consult an experienced therapist.

Goals and Objectives of Couples Therapy:

The main purpose of counseling is to increase the understanding of yourself, the partner, and the relationship patterns between you. As you apply new information to break dysfunctional patterns and build better ones, therapy becomes successful.

Couple therapy's main tasks are to improve the clarity about:

- The kind of life one want to build together
- The kind of partner one aspire to be to develop the kind of life and partnership you want to create
- Your individual barriers to become the kind of partner you aspire to be

- The skills and information you need to accomplish the above tasks.

Tradeoffs and Tough Choices:

To create a sustainable difference in your partnership, you need:

- A dream of the future you want to develop together
- Have a future apart from your partner, so you are not joined in the hip

- Appropriate attitudes and skills to function as a team

- Motivation to continue

- Time to evaluate progress.

There will be some hard exchange and challenging options for every person, to create the partnership you really want.

It's time for the first tradeoff. It only takes time to build a relationship that flourishes: time to be together, time to be with family, time to play, organize, nurture, relax, hang out, and prepare. This time, certain other important places-your personal or professional time-will be violated.

The second compromise relates to comfort. That means emotional security, such as going out on a limb to

42

explore new ways of thinking or doing things, listening, and being curious rather than holding in, speaking up rather than being resentfully obedient or withdrawing. In the beginning, there will be an emotional risk of taking action, but if you just keep sight of the shoreline, you will never discover different worlds. Moreover, few people are faced with the emotional comfort of whether they do not fulfill their beliefs or are faced with the implications of their actions.

Another comfort which will be questioned is the comfort of spark. Simply sustaining progress over time requires effort: being mindful of making a difference over time, remembering being more polite, sharing, appreciating, etc. Remembering and acting requires effort.

For some people, the other effort is even harder: that improves their reaction to problems. For example, if one person is hypersensitive to criticism and his / her partner is hypersensitive to feeling neglected, attempts will be made to strengthen their sensitivity, rather than hoping that the partner will stop ignoring or criticizing.

There is usually a tension in all those places between short-term gratification and the long-term objective of building a meaningful relationship. The blunt reality is that commitment is needed on each person's part in an

43

interdependent relationship to bring about a sustained change. It's like pairs of skating figures – one person can't do much of the job, and yet build an outstanding team.

Chapter 3: Specific Problematic Areas for Couples

This chapter covers all the problematic areas intruding couples or partners life in detail. What can be the chronic or unproductive arguments and how they can be ignored are also mentioned in detail.

3.1 Chronic or Unproductive Arguments

Reasons why couples have the same fights over and over:

Either you are married or in a serious relationship, you have undoubtedly found that some of your arguments never seem to be resolved. They get recycled instead. Why does this happen so commonly? So why do those circumstances almost feel unsolvable? There are three specific explanations for this:

Your parents actually taught you that working through conflicts wasn't possible:

Accidentally however, you tried to swap spouse points from your caretakers, and that's just what they did. When they disagreed, they would each dig in their heels and adamantly — and self-righteously — assert their position's supremacy, rather than trying to consider each other's viewpoint in a way that might lead to a mutually satisfactory agreement. And, then, carry back marital peace.

In short, they were terrible templates to show you how to treat social discord in your childhood. Their ability, or power, to participate in constructive negotiation of conflicts was zero. And what you eventually took away from their battles was the irreconcilable confrontations between "intimate partners." On the opposite, when your inner pressure cooker started boiling, all you could do was blow up and read the riot act to your mate. And sadly, the only way a reaction of this sort could alleviate your anger would be to leave your partner so humiliated by your outburst that they just forfeited you. Needless to say, such forced surrender can only cause more harm to whatever emotional connection between you still exists.

Furthermore, when you were a child, maybe without even being aware of it, you heard your parents endlessly "yeah, but" each other, or cross-complaint until each of them gave up even attempting to be heard. And maybe they'd go off-topic occasionally, wandering into any number of other distracting places. (At some point, they may have simply misunderstood what they were quarreling over in the first place.)

In these situations, it's fair to say that your parents lacked the problem-solving abilities of simple couples. How partners in a stand-off can fiercely end debates, or simply go silent, putting up an impenetrable, unscalable wall against further discussion. They are finally too busy or tired to continue fighting about something they are no closer to solving than when they began.

What is the solution? First of all, ask yourself: "Do You do any of that stuff [counterproductive]?"When you get angry, can you" catch "yourself in the act of mindlessly copying what your parents can routinely show before your very eyes? Once you press the buttons, you automatically respond. So what's natural, which means unconscious here, is to follow whatever your parents experienced when they were angry.

Regardless of whether you imitated their behaviors as an infant, these reactions can still be instilled into you or conditioned. And unfortunately, at times when you're feeling irritated they'll be at hand and feel very easy to you to "execute." That's just what you need to "reprogram" and it all begins with knowledge as well as "a-where-ness," so you'll still need to find out just when you get activated.

More precisely, you will need to develop the mindset that most of your disagreements in relation to each other are reconcilable. It is axiomatic that good marriages are based on compromise. So when you find a way to satisfy your conflicting desires in relation to each other, peace can be restored between the two of you. When your pessimistic attitude towards working through your differences changes from "such an effort is bound to be futile," to "resolving most of our disputes is entirely feasible" (as in "Where there is a will, there is a way"), you will discover that you and your partner's happy lives together slowly fade away seemingly impossible obstacles.

Getting angry with your partner— and them with you — is an ideal way to protect your ego when it feels under siege. Consequently, going ballistic as an almost foolproof way of safeguarding your vulnerability can become habitual:

And very little awareness of this. And once you know that the actions of your companion make you feel insecure at a rather primal stage, you may be motivated to physically assault (or counter-attack) them. Interestingly, whether the discrepancies in your companion render you unhappy, or when you feel judged by them, aggressive response staves easily off the fear that is starting to surface from the very depths of your being.

We just ought to look forward to ourselves. If anyone else questions for our morality, honesty, intellect, such positive emotions for oneself may quickly sound challenged. Until when you are thoroughly self-validating, so that you're not taking too hard to heart by another's derogatory judgment, you'll be obligated to ward off some perceived threat or indignity instantly.

This all-too-fiery emotion is the only emotion that "immunizes" you with feelings of weakness. And once you raise your finger, you pass onto someone some leftover bad emotions about yourself that would otherwise intrude: "They're to blame, they're at wrong— surely not me!"

In these situations, you're encouraged to smash under the belt — often far below the belt. You suspect the companion with some sort of nastiness you might think of; rudely challenge them; negatively attach the harshest, most uncomplimentary intentions to them; give them (unsolicited) a singularly unflattering "diagnosis" of behavior; nail them with a preference (possibly fourletter) label; ride the morally superior "high-horse" and condescendingly lecture to them regarding their shortcomings; Patronize or mock them; make demands or ultimatums apt to humiliate or appeal to them; and so on.

Additionally, when you're fighting another human (most definitely your partner, since it's usually your most fragile relationship), you're infected by the stress response recognized as "fight or flight." And the whole-body preparation of this agitated state generates adrenaline it, physically reinforcing you, gives you a sense of power and control that, only seconds before, might have been intensely ignored. This would give you a clear sense of how unintentionally enticing indignation can be with its special capacity to keep crippling self-doubts from the history submerged.

The problem with frustration is that it stops you from really responding to grievances from your companion who could be very legitimate and warrant the utmost consideration. Probably, if you both disagree, you can guarantee that none of you listens to the other really carefully. Because that's literally key to what frustration "accomplishes": it helps you to break from an anxiety-causing listening environment because you're completely concentrated on marshaling the facts against your "clearly-in - thewrong" companion.

The protective posture is shared in way too many situations. Both you and your mate are going on the offensive by psychologically motivating yourself by indignation, while what you're really doing is simply protecting against an inherent insecurity that you might have very little knowledge of — or insight into.

What is the solution? What's required here is for you to improve your confidence and learn how to justify yourself. Realize that in most instances, the judgment of your friend regards them as much as it regards you, and you alone claim the right to assess yourself, so you should do it kindly — with consideration, empathy, so acceptance. And then do you no longer have to focus on the rage to protect yourself from the harsh judgment of someone.

Note, too, that the hormonal, sensitive portion of the brain can control you until you're ready to calm off. When your marital issues are to be resolved effectively, you may need to put aside your legitimate point of view to reflect on the contrasting viewpoint of your spouse, to do so with respect and compassion. So agreeing with the role of your mate, so appreciating its abstract value —

just though you misidentify from your own — can mitigate most of your rage itself.

There are certain core differences between the two of you — either because of your natures or your ideologies — and they're simply not resolvable:

The condition therefore accounts for the ongoing stalemates. Such irresolvable inconsistencies may be adjusted, acclimatized, or consented to, but they cannot be changed or rendered consistent. If the excessive extroversion of your spouse often gets on your nerves because they still want to go out and do something, while you're basically an introvert — a home girl, happy to follow your passions comfortably, and putter about the house on your own — your spouse may well say, "What's wrong with you? You will never want something to say! "You might be made to gripe in return," Why do we have to go out all the time? What's wrong with just staying at home with the children and me? Aren't we enough for you? "

Based on your anatomy, you're just going to require more or less additional stimuli than the other. It's something you simply can't control, and complaining over it mainly applies to each of you thinking like who your companion is invalidating who you are, anyway.

This is sort of crazy — or at least crazymaking, if you think about it. You're not thinking about morals or vices, but you're asking about human predilections. So since you have a pronounced affinity for candy, it's not reasonable to object to your partner's desire for, say, and vanilla ice cream. Perhaps irrationally, however, all of us feel disturbed by these unchangeable discords.

Nevertheless, particular values that have crystallized over time are persistent, if not inherently endearing — and practically unchangeable. Even many people with highly discrepant views can't resist blaming each other for keeping so tight to a role they can't appeal to themselves — or may simply hate one another. Perhaps one explanation people will constantly struggle over political discrepancies is that the disparity in their partner's views causes them a disconcerting feeling in isolation. If their irreconcilable beliefs refer to religion, theological belief, or something else, such disagreements will inevitably become a prickly thorn in the side of a partnership.

What is the solution? The solution for grid locking such a partnership would be evident. If there are things you and your wife can never actually decide about, it's better to literally exclude them from the discussion — unless, that is, one of you is consciously reconsidering values you once considered sacrosanct. But no matter how openminded you might be on other things, it's always possible that you've agreed "definitely" about certain issues. Yet, unfortunately, the spouse has the same. And if both of you are close-minded, it's important that each of you learn to understand and accept these unchanging variations.

Note, you will remove everything, until now, has caused you too much gratuitous discomfort as you start embracing such discomfiting aspects in your partner's make-up or learned values.

Tell yourself: "Which option is that?"This just brings some space between you to look down on your mate for having views contradictory to yourself. So the isolation may conflict with the desire, or inclination, to interact with them in person. If your spouse derives important emotional encouragement from their religious observance, for example, will you affirm this as essential to them and graciously acknowledge the truth, even if you might be a convinced atheist yourself? It's definitely no easy feat. But if you can see their philosophy as not undermining your own, acknowledging a discrepancy that you'd certainly rather wasn't the case would be far easier.

It's likely to fall into a fight with your mate occasionally, but that never implies the realistic alternatives aren't close at hand. This is just a question of having the desire to bring them into action.

3.2 Verbal Abuse

In a partnership, verbal abuse happens from nowhere. It becomes even more cynical and manipulative, leading people to doubt themselves on the receiving end, worrying whether they are overreacting or even blaming themselves. Typically verbal harassment happens in private areas where no one else may interfere and gradually becomes a normal mode of contact within a relationship. To those who suffer it, verbal harassment is mostly marginalized, and it eats away at your self-esteem, finding it impossible to reach out to a mate.

Many people who witness it in their head rationalize the violence and don't really know it's an inappropriate method of contact. But this doesn't make those on the receiving end any less distressing or emotionally taxing. Basically, verbal violence is a tool in order to retain dominance and authority over someone. There are a number of various types that verbal violence can take, rendering it much more challenging to understand. Of starters, verbal harassment involves being exposed to name-calling on a daily basis, feeling continually demeaned or belittled, and being subjected to a partner's silent treatment.

When you can't say if your companion is "funny" or "belittling," here are a number of say-tale indications that your partnership is deteriorating.

11 most common verbal abuse patterns:

These are the 11 most common verbal abuse patterns to look out for in a relationship:

1. Name-calling:

This kind of verbal violence is perhaps the most readily identifiable. This involves being named names and/or getting yelled at constantly. Arguments that often turn to shouting in a debate and utilizing offensive words are both indicators that your relationship with your spouse is anything but safe. Partners back away from a dispute in a stable partnership, or seek to talk about the problem. The offender can scream in a verbally abusive partnership unless they get what they want.

Example: "You fool, you have made me angry now!

2. Condescension:

Subtle sarcasm and a cynical tone of voice need not be a regular feature of the companion relationships. It can also mean being the frequent object of laughs from the mate. It may start sweet, which is why it always goes undetected, but in the course of time, condescension is abominable.

Example: "No wonder your weight is still complaining, look how clean your plate is!

3. Manipulation:

Often detecting a manipulative personality can be simple, particularly when someone constantly forces their spouse to do something they're not really happy with to do. By comparison, deception may be difficult to spot. It can be subtle, like flipping around circumstances and laying the blame on the person being victimized.

Example: "If you truly liked me, you wouldn't say that, or you wouldn't do that."

4. Criticism:

It's OK to have positive criticism when questioned on occasion; it's good to be frank with your mate. Nevertheless, persistent disappointment and belittling of a significant other is NOT good and may result in a substantial loss of self-esteem over time.

Example: "Why do you get so disorganized? I can count on you many times for destroying our nights out!

5. Demeaning comments:

This is dangerous if a companion puts you down using demeaning remarks relating to your race / ethnic heritage, class, faith, history, in general. This need not need to be systematic, if it occurs once, it would certainly happen again, and would not be minimized. A companion that likes you and values you won't use something that's innate in you to bring you down.

Examples: "I'm not shocked, you're Asian, you're all doing that" or "you girls, weeping for nothing as useless cries."

6. Threats:

While that may be an easy one to know, it's not always the case. Threats may be done up in a way that lets them sound as though they're "not that serious," or in a manner that makes you doubt whether you've heard it correct. Yet a danger is a hazard, and they are not resorted to by a romantic friend to get their way.

Examples: "I'm going to injure myself if you're leaving me tonight" or "If you don't do this, you might notice your cat is outside spending the night!"

7. Blame:

Blame is one of the most prevalent types of verbal violence, which entails continually imposing the blame on a spouse for one's behavior rather than accepting responsibility for them. These might involve punishing a person over events that they have nothing to do about, punishing the spouse for the actions of the victim.

Examples: "You are the cause we're never on schedule! And" See what you've done to me now! "

8. Accusations:

Repeated allegations sometimes arising from extreme envy are a type of verbal assault. Being continually suspected of something also causes a person to start wondering whether they are doing anything wrong / inappropriately dressing/speaking too often, etc.

Examples: "I bet you are deceiving on me! "Or, "I noticed you flirting with your manager again when I was talking with your dull teammates."

9. Withholding:

A spouse can often step away from a confrontation, choosing to allow the dust to settle and partake in a more meaningful discussion without flaring up emotions. While that is certainly a hallmark of a good relationship, the silent treatment, also called withholding, which is not. Withholding can involve your companion failing to reply to your calls if they don't get what they want, or avoiding you outright.

Example: You are debating choices for restaurants because you don't want to go for your partner's option. They're leaving the room and declining to speak to you because you're "bad."

10. Gas lighting:

Gas lighting means discounting the desires of a person and having them question whether their thoughts are insignificant and/or fake. This is a very popular sort of emotional violence which, since it can be subtle, which highly coercive, sometimes goes undetected. Gas lighting will render you feel lonely and incapable of voicing your feelings. Gas lighted individuals frequently catch themselves, sorry for actions they never performed.

Examples: "Why are you so focused on everything?

11. Circular Arguments:

When your companion continually disputes with you and fights if they find an opening or if talks and debates continue to go round in circles, making you exhausted and depressed, then these are both indicators of a dysfunctional partnership. Those on the receiving end of these sorts of disputes appear to sound like they're sitting on eggshells and stop coming back again and again to the same point. We don't necessarily need to compromise to everything in a partnership, but that can be agreed collectively, rather than an environment of one-using the other or participating in debates you will never gain.

You may be in an unstable partnership if you sound like you're always on the verge and walking on eggshells with your mate, or if any of those habits feel old to you. Often, if your trustworthy buddies and/or relatives inform you anything is wrong, please listen to them. They can see or hear what you can't understand. Note, you can learn to support yourself in a partnership by establishing limits, and being frank about how it makes you feel.

3.3 Separating work from Home Life

Job – Family dispute is not an individual occurrence, but can influence everyone, including family members and coworkers/supervisors, around them. However, analysis has concentrated mainly on workrelated effects – relationship dispute on an entity basis, rather than from a dyadic, social, or corporate level. There is increasing literature on the convergence burden of job – family disputes with others. The mechanisms by which these systems occur, and the long-term convergence tension effects for others, remain unknown, however. Researchers ought to raise deeper questions regarding how the role of parent's job-family tension impacts children over the span of life-from adolescence through adulthood. Scholars will need to discuss how one spouse's job-family dispute influences the everyday lives and emotional wellbeing of another.

Finally, organizational research will also challenge how work-family tension interactions influence person and group-level dynamics between coworkers. More generally, such kinds of research will help explain the wider effect of practice – family dispute on culture.

In the term work-family dispute, the concept of 'family' must be extended to encompass alternate social types and behaviors beyond the commonly established nuclear family. Job – Family rivalry with small children is often synonymous with the conventional portrayal of the dual-career pair. Unmarried nonparents globally, however, often encounter work-family tension dependent on the responsibilities to those within one's social network, such as extended family members, friends, and neighbors. In fact, the concept of what constitutes family may incorporate alternate types of marriage, such as pairs of same-sex with and without children. Job analysis – family dispute – including concepts and methodology of study – ought to develop to include such less prevalent interactions.

The effect of Occupational conditions:

Evidence suggests that the work-family dispute relationship is influenced by working circumstances and the atmosphere of the workforce. Others claim that working environments will have a greater difference than the real amount of hours employed. Particularly significant are flexibility and power over schedules and task material, which are not only correlated with employee fulfillment and occupational wellbeing but have also been shown to alleviate tension between work and family. For example, workplace autonomy was correlated with higher rates of work-family balance for both men and women.

Supportive bosses, exposure to insurance, and the opportunity to choose family-friendly choices are all critical in this matter, which may help parents properly handle conflicting jobs which family demands. Often prevalent in the careers and corporate world, the organizational culture which demands full time and energy commitment to the job may be a serious obstacle to family life. Indeed, becoming productive implies staying childless for some people in the top positions, especially women.

On the other side, non-standard operating hours have proved to be counterproductive. Rotating and night shifts are correlated with greater marital dysfunction and tension between the working and home. Shift employment is often a source of tension for single moms, not just because of elevated rates of physical discomfort, but also because these kinds of occupations make it tougher for them to find childcare, thus raising tension and parental responsibility for the wellbeing of their babies.

The downside among single parents often derives from the reality that they are far more inclined than most parents to job non-standard work hours. Since they are usually younger and less well-educated, single parents are more likely to focus in low-status job sectors with stressful and restrictive schedules, have less flexibility over the work cycle, and provide little advantages, if any. Single parents are also especially prone to extreme time-squeezes.

3.4 Sexual issues and Problems

The fact is that, when it comes to sex, both men and women continue to talk about the same issues, particularly while they are in a long-term relationship. Below are eight of the most popular concerns generally receive from partners, along with tips for flipping upside down a partner's frown.

1. Laziness:

When the spouse has started doing their sharing between the sheets, seek a discreet solution instead. Playfully lament how much you enjoy turning his or her signature in bed, be it a switch, twist, or move. A gentle note that tango needs two may be all it takes. When this doesn't fit, then opt with a straighter solution. Inform your companion politely that you found he or she is not displaying the same effort, and inquire why. If there is no reason (and if you're confident there are no medical issues), be frank about how his or her lack of enthusiasm in bed sometimes takes the pleasure out of sex for you. When your partner is involved in your partnership, he or she steps up to the challenge with love. In the meantime, revising your own rambunctiousness may be a pleasant idea. A lazy companion, in or out of bed, isn't worth the effort.

2. Boredom:

Can you schedule your watch when he is going to hand you over? See her touch fall a mile away? Long term sex will gradually become easy to predict with the same individual. So while there's something soothing about physical intimacy, if it's the only meal on the table, it may foster disdain. Experiment with different positions to get out of bedroom isolation, focus on improving your physical abilities, or shock your lover by asking him or her an intimate vision or a filthy dream to kick-start your romantic imaginations. Change the way you treat yourself in bed. Normally, if you are silent, wake up the neighbors. If you happen to be loud, dial it down. Take the pace, if you're usually sluggish and steady. Place a sex toy under the pillow of your spouse, whether it is a high-tech vibrator, a feather tickler, or a heating/cooling lubricant for extra vibration.

3. Ignoring the connection between EmotionalPhysical intimacies:

The manner in which a pair view each other outside the bedroom affects the quality of their love life strongly. Nasty, nagging, and disruptive spouses rarely enjoy the ultimate relationship. Strengthen the connection by improving contact, prioritizing a couple of times, letting your partner feel valued, and following the attitude of modesty, open-mindedness, and a team player. Replace the criticism or disdain with a polite, affectionate sound in your speech. Do the "small stuff" you think it will be making your companion get a happy day. It is your best bet for a more hot night.

4. Electronic interlopers:

Laptops, computers, I-Products, and smart phones provide a way to get into the bedroom and eminimize private downtime for a couple. When you respond to a text or change your Facebook status instead of snuggling your sweetheart, you unwittingly send out the impression that your companion is not as fascinating or significant as the individual on the other side of whatever device is in your hand. Render your dormitory a technology-free space. Charge the kitchen counter on your mobile phone and drop your device in the living room.

Reclaim your double suite.

5. A negative body image:

In long-term marriages, improvements in the body are expected. When there are female, they get pregnant and give birth. They are speeding up. They are adding weight and losing their eyes. Health issues and the everyday pressures are now taking a toll on the body. The health rates are increasing and falling down. Such shifts may cause people to become self-conscious about their bodies, causing them to cover up more and have a little intercourse. Couples should adopt a healthy lifestyle for improving body image. As especially, they will tend to complement the beauty and desirability of each other. Beauty truly is in the beholder's eye.

6. Disparate sex drives:

If you're the one with an inherently higher sex desire, don't annoy your mate, moan when you don't understand it, mock their lower desire or try to have sex somewhere. Act like an individual. If your drive is incredibly strong, the burden off your companion be lifted by some "alone time." Recognize that there is a link between physical and emotional affection, whether you are the one with the lower drive, and that the fair and caring demands for sex from your spouse are vital to your relationship as a happy, long term couple. No magic number remains. The secret to this is harmony.

7. Missing the Connection between Mental and Physical Arousal:

Many guides on intimacy highlight the value of improved approaches, different poses, and sex toys, all items that help you feel stronger. That's awesome, but the calculation is just half that. Couples will always work on activating the strongest sex organ — the brain. Sex is at its strongest, while couples are switched on emotionally as well as physically. One of the writer blends the visual eroticism of the 50 Shades of Grey genre with kinky "how to" sex tips in his new novel, 50 Ways to Play: BDSM for Decent People, which will help traditional lovers transform their dreams into actual play in the bedroom.

8. Exhaustion:

True old-fashioned exhaustion is a key concern among the active couples in today's bedroom. Tackle the bedtime ritual as a team to overcome it. Ask what you should do to help cool down your companion without going out. You should finish the supper dishes, put the kids in bed, or allow the companion some space to complete his or her job papers. If you have identical habits, so you will go to bed at the same moment. It not only improves the odds of remaining together but also tells the spouse you are in it together.

Here are further 11 more interrupting issues regarding sex between couples and some of their compensations:

1. Female clients frequently claim they are too busy to be through intercourse at the time. It is especially true of many mothers, because the parental strain will block some sexy thoughts. It might seem counterintuitive but it will help to plan age. When you realize when it can happen, you may be more prepared to adapt to it. Alternatively, adding any excitement by sex instruments or different sex styles will serve to hold you alive and present.

2. That story of how unfeeling, sex-obsessed robots are doing a disservice for dudes. Men sometimes feel confused by this idea that they are sentimental

70

Neanderthals. Some show that they really want to get better inside and outside the bed, but they really don't know how. Make things easy for him by being open to a monkey see through your own emotions; monkey does complex. When he feels mushy, you should still be super affectionate — it's just about constructive reinforcement.

3. If one individual feels the other doesn't have enough of the good times to go, anger will bubble up. Waiting for your mate to start and getting upset when it doesn't happen, then you should do something while you're in the mood. Stop selfishness from destroying your partnership. And if you're on the other end of the spectrum, realize that the appeal your companion makes for you to initiate intercourse more frequently is just about feeling wanted, and making that initiative will massively strengthen your relationship.

4. At happy hour you may have noticed this one across the table because if it relates to you, you know how annoying it can be. When you're in the heat of the moment, it's better to literally remind your mate what's important for you by putting their hand in the right places. When you're going to talk out, it's good to phrase what you expect in a constructive manner as. You appreciate it so much when the partner is doing XYZ because it sounds less of a suggestion and more of promoting what they're actually doing.

5.   Luckily, this has a humorous remedy. Every day, you can tell each other one thing you admire about the other person. If that's too bad for your tastes, add the little gestures that you originally depended on to express intimacy when you first started dating: holding hands, throwing your arms around each other when seated together, touching each other's necks, etc.

6.   Although it's cool if both parties are in it only for the physical release, if you want an emotional bond but don't sense it, things get more turbid. That is what "empty species," which doesn't sound very interesting. To further banish the sensation, function outside of the bedroom to encourage intimacy. Spend more time together, discover fresh, simple experiences that will help you build a connection and seek different ways to offer joy to you and to your companion.

7.   When a straight pair attempts to conceive, the guy may feel like he is working on the order. When you're ovulating, there will be a compromise between articulating   and   spontaneity.

Communication is crucial to deciding whether to cross this boundary, because certain male partners would want to learn every aspect of your period, and some would like to remain less sensitive to the details. And if the end objective is to reproduce, no matter when he falls, you also will put a sense of anticipation back into sex. Doing stuff like wearing lingerie and sending sexy messages will help make a baby seem enjoyable, rather than a burden.

8. While the lack of sleep and tension will send serious walloping to the sex drive, it's not all gone. There are a number of people that since beginning a family were willing to restore a satisfying dating existence. Find out whether logistical would deter you from feeling happy or whether the question is just physical in the first place. It also has something to do with unexpressed or unmet social communication and affection requirements. One way to access the real problem is to arrange an appointment with a psychiatrist who would be willing to speak to you all about it.

9. Feeling that your companion doesn't understand that you're destroying your link to each other, which just makes the situation worse. There are couples discussing this clearly in counseling, instead of dancing around the subject. Lets imagine an example: We need to say, 'I feel like Y when you do

X,' because there's no space for confusion. Such declarations regarding" I "are important to making your spouse not feel threatened.

10. If there ever had been a moment to tread carefully, it should have been it. While premature ejaculation becomes a problem at the outset of the relationship — except with the very first potential nervousness — it happens as a whole problem. When you two have sex for the first time, an expert suggests that you hold your confusing emotions under control and pass on, either to other activities, whether he's up for it or to anything non-sexual. When it occurs again, that is an issue that doesn't go anywhere. Gently persuade him to visit a specialist and make sure there is no underlying reason to get some guidance about what's going to help his body cope while it's raring to go.

11. Once the honeymoon period has faded off this one also forces its way through relationship. The person who desires more of sex may feel neglected, but without a conversation, their spouse does not know it. Luckily, adjustments will save the day. Discuss how much you would like to

be sexually involved together and hammer out a schedule in the middle ground. Set dates you've always decided to be romantic and make a running list of items you'd want to check out.

Experimenting on what's turning on will help you look forward to having good sex back.3.5 In-Laws Controversies

At any point, most families are dealing with in-law problems. Of starters, you may feel that your in-laws don't support you, or your partner is too dismissive of them. And they have an opinion on everything that goes from where you stay to how you raise your babies.

Having problems with your in-laws doesn't mean that you are in an abusive partnership.

It is similar to war. Conflicting doesn't ruin a partnership. Yet they will do things poorly. So the same is out with the in-law challenges. What counts is how such problems are treated.

Here's how balanced couples treat with their in-laws.

Healthy couples realize their in-laws are unique people:

Healthy families are coping with their in-laws and understanding that they are special individuals in many respects.

The families have a nature of their own. Healthy partners know that society is "not incorrect or evil, just special."

Healthy couples make an effort regarding their in-laws:

They know the role their in-laws play in the life of their partner. They handle them politely. They join social functions. They "require their in-laws access to their families." In other words, they make an attempt, even if "they do not necessarily approve, appreciate the complexities, practices or customs of the families, or even look forward to the future together."

Healthy couples set cool boundaries with their in-laws:

They should have frank discussions regarding their desires with their partners and build a roadmap on which all of them consent. For example: Your partner is Cool with his mom coming by an unannounced. You really don't. And you agree that you ought to contact family members beforehand and make sure it's a pleasant moment to come over.

Healthy couples distinct their own relationship from their in-laws:

And they are not contracted to them, no matter how confusing or unpleasant their in-laws can be.

And when the in-laws are extremely challenging to contend with, happy people make a special attempt to be good to their spouse. They might say "I love you" or execute a nice gesture.

Healthy couples distinct their spouse from their in-laws:

For e.g., Mom might be invasive and dismissive of a man, but a happy couple knows that her conduct may not represent how the guy thinks regarding the stuff she reflects on.

Healthy couples keep communicating:

Term-processing is one of the most critical techniques a pair has to negotiate with in-laws. So they are thinking about their own positions. They are attentive. They fully sympathize with the emotions of each other.

Healthy couples don't take it personally:

A stable pair will understand and cope with the reality that their parents are human beings, with natural and complicated human emotions. They are seeking to learn where they come from, so they're empathizing.

Tips for Dealing with In-Laws:

Here are further five suggestions for dealing with your in-laws:

Set boundaries:

Define the boundaries you want to establish for your in-laws. For e.g., if your mother-in-law is taking over your kitchen each time she comes, speak to your spouse about it. Then have a polite yet straightforward talk with her about the problem.

You might suggest the following: "Mother, we love that you do care and want to help us out by doing some cooking and know that you really enjoy it, but we would appreciate if you let Mary (wife) take the lead in our kitchen. If you want to help, she would really appreciate if you are willing to create the salad for dinner tonight."

Remember it's only an opinion:

Remembering so much of what we are taught is an idea, not fact, helps. And if your mother-in-law recommends that you can feed your son with a different diet, note that you don't have to accept it, fight it out of existence or view it as a critique of you. Although we can't avoid talking to an in-law, we can regulate how we hear them.

Remember your in-laws are people:

They are like you, have desires, fears, suspicions, and emotions. Treat them not as guardians, just like all other individuals you slowly become acquainted with.

Respect your spouse's attachments:

It helps to consider the commitment of the husband to his kin as something to be valued. For starters, if the regular calls your husband makes to his father are valuable to him, it is therefore valuable for you to recognize and acknowledge that.

Take deep breaths:

Take a pause to relax as you are about to hit a breaking point. Find a peaceful spot, like a bathroom or taking a stroll. When you relax, reflect on the good qualities of your in-laws — such as "they just enjoy our family" — and note that you can't influence or alter them.

Your in-laws are important to your family, and they're part of your life. It is up to you all to find a way to make your time as fun as possible with extended family.

Chapter 4: The Georama; a Window into the Psyche

What does a window into the psyche means and how to enter into someone's psyche, how to understand someone truly, are all the major concern of this chapter? What is a Johari's window into psyche and how this concept works on practical basis is also mentioned in detail?

4.1 Johari's window into Psyche

Johari's window is a term used in psychology to describe the interpersonal interaction awareness. It takes its name from its inventors Joseph Luft and Harry Ingham. Sometimes represented as a diagram of a two-by-two square format. This represents the four conceivable variations of what is common to itself and unfamiliar to others. Let's look at how Johari's window relates to cases when you are exchanging your picture with someone. We will start with the upper left window pane.

1. Known to Self / Known to Other:

Let's assume, as some see the picture; they're giving feedback on it. They may tell something about their subject matter, their artistic quality, the methods used to produce it, or a concept that is being articulated. If you decide to nod your head, since you realize such details and presumably meant them, then that is the first pane of Johari's window: items regarding the picture that are known to yourself and others. Psychologists consider the quadrant

"accessible."

It would be a fulfilling feeling much of the way. You also developed the picture with a particular intent in mind, and people see it. That's what picture sharing is all about: Contact effectively. The more images you exchange of someone, the larger the quadrant is.

2. Known to Self / Unknown to Other:

If we move over to the top right window, we find ourselves in a position that is not normally so satisfying. People are not conscious of the concept that you are trying to convey in the picture. They don't note the methods that you were using. They really don't get it and you that end up feeling unappreciated, disappointed, and confused – particularly if you attempted to convey a specific thinking or feeling in the picture.

So what? Okay, you may believe that your picture struggled to connect, and you go back to the drawing board to start again. Or clarify the photo. You could also "self-disclose," as they suggest in behavioral communication, to make others appreciate the particular thinking or emotion you were attempting to express. When it succeeds, and they see it now, you managed to move back to the first screen successfully.

Others can may often be conscious of the intent and attempts to produce the shot, but they really don't know much about it. In this scenario, a little investigation on your side can make you know that you're still in a condition of Pane # 1 – but it will certainly be good for people to identify what they understand without needing to check to find out. Users might not know anything about the picture of certain cases because you are purposely not asking them. Perhaps there is something sensitive about the snapshot you'd rather not share, perhaps it contains one of your visual secrets. And psychologists often term this the quadrant "secret."

3. Unknown to Self / Known to Other:
Let's pass on to the window below left. It is here where things begin to get interesting in this "blank" quadrant. People spot facets of your picture that you haven't seen, even though you've put a lot of thought and energy into making the image sometimes. If the individual points out

a mistake, it may be quite confusing, as though you didn't see the power pole stretching out of the head of the topic. It is a reminder of how the blind spots will form in your eye.

On the other hand, people could point to something positive about the person you didn't believe yourself to be. Perhaps it's in the structure, or the thought being articulated. Images can be so nuanced and delicate you can't catch it. You also randomly miss a significant aspect that made it a decent shot.

Lightbulbs often start flashing in your head as people who are mentally astute interpret something in the picture regarding your temperament or lifestyle even when you didn't want to disclose it. They would claim in interpersonal psychology that "feedback" from the other individual caused an idea for you. You have now passed back to Pane # 1, with that perspective, whilst on the way feeling an empathic link with that guy.

This is one of the consequences of posting photos and can be very interesting, though often also a little overwhelming. We're not really aware of the hidden influences influencing our images. When we consider the point of view of other citizens, the problem might be difficult for them too. Will you find out something in a picture when the photographer obviously doesn't know it? What are you doing?

4. Unknown to Self / Unknown to Other:

The last pane in the window of Johari, to the lower right, is the most enigmatic. This is quadrant "unknown." Is there anything significant in your picture that you do not remember, not the other person? Perhaps you just didn't take the time or have no eye to note something important about the idea, composition, or technique. Or maybe there is something that's so vague or secret in your appearance that neither of you will see it.

So how do you realize the difference in a circumstance in which anything significant is secret to self and others and a case in which nothing significant is to be known?

You really don't. That is why this quadrant is apparently "hidden." Only by discussing the picture with someone, through self-disclosure and input, can you find out. The cycle may take you to Pane # 3, where the other individual begins to know more about the picture you don't yet have. This might move to Pane # 2, where you have a glimpse into your job when the other individual doesn't yet. If the purpose of imaging is to connect effectively with others, and also inside your own mind, the cycle hopefully leads back to Pane # 1, where all of you acquire a deeper interpretation of the picture and what it represents.

4.2   How to observe someone's Psyche?

This is not about having understood minds like Twilight's Edward Cullen. That can only be achieved by vampires (if they do exist).

It's about understanding what many people like to be doing, without terms. It's about knowing what they actually want, even though they're pretending something.

The ability to interpret people correctly can influence your emotions, family, and work-life dramatically.

When you realize how another person thinks, so you will adapt your message and conversation style to ensure that it is handled in the best possible way.

It is not that difficult. This may sound cliché, but no special abilities are required to learn how to read minds.

So, here's 16 ideas for reading people like a top player:

1. Be objective and open-minded:

You have to first practice keeping an open mind before you begin to understand others. Don't let your previous perceptions and feelings affect your thoughts and views.

If you quickly evaluate people, it can lead you to misread others. Be analytical in moving closer to any encounter and circumstance.

Logic alone won't tell you the entire tale of someone. You have to yield to certain critical sources of knowledge, and you can learn to interpret the essential non-verbal, intuitive signals people send out. You have to remain impartial to interpret details neutrally without distorting it to actually understand others.

2. Pay attention to appearance:

We have to consider people's presence while interpreting something. What is it they wear?

Were they suited up for results, showing that they are ambitious? And carry jeans and a t-shirt which implies comfort?

Do they have a pendant that shows their Christian beliefs, such as a cross or Buddha? Everything they carry, everything you can infer from it.

You should pay attention to "identity statements."

There are items that people want to reveal in their clothes, like a t-shirt in logos, badges, or bands.

Identity declarations are intentional comments we're creating regarding our beliefs, aspirations, principles, etc. One of the aspects that are really important to keep in mind about identity statements is because they're explicit, sometimes people assume we're exploiting them, and we're disingenuous, but there's little evidence to suggest that's going on. The citizens just want to be recognized, generally. They'll also do that to the downside of looking good. If it comes down to the decision, they would rather be viewed authentically than favorably.

Also, certain studies indicate that maybe personality characteristics may have been interpreted on a person's face – to some degree.

Higher rates of extraversion were correlated with more protruding nose and tongue, recessive chin muscles, and masseter muscles (muscles used in chewing). In comparison, the face of people with lower degrees of Extraversion displayed the opposite effect, as the skin around the nose tended to rub towards the forehead. These results indicate that somehow personality characteristics may be read on a person's face to some degree, but further research will be required to explain this phenomenon.

3. Pay attention to people's posture:

The stance of one human tells a lot about his or her personality. Holding their head up indicates they are comfortable. This could be a symptom of poor selfesteem, whether they move indecisively or cower.

When it comes to stance, check at whether they are keeping their high in a relaxed way, or if they are walking indecisively or cowering, which suggests poor self-confidence.

4. Watch their physical movements:

By gestures, people convey their emotions rather than words. For instance, we tilt towards things we want, and away from others, we don't.

When they reach back when their hands are out and free, palms facing up, it's a positive indication they're interacting with you. Unless you've seen the person leaning forward, it indicates that he or she is constructing a structure. The passing of arms or legs is another step to consider. That indicates defensiveness, rage, or self-protection if you see a person doing this.

When someone turns over, and you say something all of a sudden and their arms crossed, so you realize you said what this person didn't like. Covering one's face, on the other side, implies they're covering something. But if you see them chewing their lips or removing their cuticles, it implies they want to soothe themselves under strain or in an uncomfortable position.

5. Try to interpret facial expressions:

If you're a poker face expert, the feelings are branded on your lips.

There are many approaches to view the facial features. These are: When you see deep frown lines emerging, the individual may be worried or overthinking.

At the opposite, a person who is genuinely laughing reveals the feet of the crow – the lines of happiness that smile. One thing to watch out for is pursed lips that may show resentment, contempt, or bitterness. A tight jaw and grinding of teeth are indicators of stress, too.

A description of smiles are as follows:

 Reward smile: Lips pushed outward immediately, mouth side dimples and eyebrows raise. This gives constructive reviews.

Affiliate smile: includes pushing the lips close when creating tiny dimples on the mouth hand as well— Mark of love and affection.

Dominance smile: The upper lip becomes lifted, and the lips are pulled forward, the forehead is wrinkled, the face and mouth indentation deepens, and the upper lids are extended.

6. Don't run away from small talk:

You may feel awkward with the small talk. It may also offer you the opportunity to get acquainted with the other guy.

Small talk lets you understand how an individual acts under regular circumstances. You will also use that as a guide to reliably detect some out of the ordinary behavior.

The author points out a variety of mistakes people create in attempting to understand others, and one of them is that they don't have a reference for how they usually behave.

7. Scan the person's overall behavior:

We also presume that if an action is taken, such as looking down at the floor during a discussion, it implies that the individual is nervous or anxious. So if you're acquainted with a person already, you'll know if the person is avoiding eye contact or simply relaxed as he or she stares down the hall.

People have various traits and action habits, and some of these behaviors might only be mannerisms.

This is why it would benefit you to establish a model of the typical actions of others.

Know how to recognize some divergence from the normal actions of an individual. When you detect a difference in their sound, rhythm, or body language, you'll realize something is wrong.

8.   Ask clear questions to get a straight answer:

You have to keep away from the unclear queries to get a clear answer. Often pose questions that require a clear answer.

Mind to not disturb the question while the individual is responding. Alternatively, you should examine the mannerisms of the individual when they talk.

Looking for "words of action" to provide an idea into how someone thinks: For starters if the manager decides she's decided to go with brand X, the word of action is fixed. This single term suggests that the manager 1) is most definitely not impulsive, 2) has considered several choices, and 3) thought stuff through words of practice give insights into a person's way of thinking.

9. Notice the words and tone used:

Learn to remember the words they use while you are talking to others. When they claim, "This is my second bonus," they want you to realize that they had already won a bonus too.

Think what? Such kinds of individuals depend on others to improve their self-image. They want you to give them attention, and they feel confident about themselves.

Our speech sound and intensity will say a great deal about our emotions. The wavelengths of sound produce vibrations. Note how the tone of voice influences you while hearing others. Ask yourself: Does it sound calming in their tone? Or is it snippy, abrasive, or whiny?

10. Listen to what your gut says:

Particularly listen to your gut when you first come across a human. This can give you a gut response before you have a chance to reflect.

Whether you're at peace with the guy or not, your heart can transmit.

Rapidly, gut feelings arise a primitive reaction. These are your inner meter of reality, relaying whether you can trust men.

11. Feel the goosebumps, if any:

Goosebumps happen when people who move or inspire us to resonate. When an individual says something that hits a chord inside us, it may also happen.

When we look at research [on the chills], outside the evolutionary response to warming ourselves, it's music that appears to trigger it, as well as moving experiences and even films.

Additionally, when we experience Deja-vu, we feel it, a recognition that you knew somebody before, even though you have never actually met.

12. Pay attention to flashes of insight:

You can have a feeling of "ah-ha" for people occasionally. Yet remain cautious as these ideas come in a light.

We tend to miss it because we are going so quickly on to the next thought that these critical insights are lost.

Intestinal feelings are the internal meter of truth: "Intestinal feelings arise quickly, a visceral reaction. They become your inner reality meter, relaying whether you should trust others.

13. Sense the person's presence:

This means that we have to sense the total social environment around us.

If you interpret individuals, seek to remember whether the individual has a nice personality that draws you or you face a wall, causing you back off.

Presence is the total energy we produce, not inherently congruent with words or behavior.

14. Watch people's eyes:

They say our eyes are the gateway to our hearts – they convey strong energies. Hence take the opportunity to study people's pupils. When you look, do you see a loving soul? Are they rude, upset, or guarded?

Eyes will convey that we are pretending or telling the truth. They can even serve as a strong indicator about what people like when looking at pupil scale.

15. Don't make assumptions:

It almost goes without saying, but remember in mind the misunderstandings stem from assumptions. If you make conclusions quickly without really meeting the guy, this can create further trouble.

There are some errors that people create while interpreting someone, and one of them was not conscious of prejudices. If you believe, for example, that your friend is mad, so whatever they say or do would look to you as disguised rage.

Do not leap to a conclusion because your wife goes to bed early, instead of enjoying your favorite television series. She may just be lazy-don't presume she's not involved in sharing time with you. Relaxing and holding the mind free and optimistic is the secret to reading others like a pro.

16. Practice watching people:

Practice makes us better, and the more examples you learn, the more likely people become to be understood.

Seek to practice watching talk shows on silence as an activity. Looking at their facial gestures and behavior can let you see what people mean when they talk, without hearing any sentences. Then watch with the volume on again to see if your conclusion is right.

More elaboration of the techniques used in the Art of Reading People:

Observe Body Language Cues:

Studies have found that words constitute just 7 percent of how we talk, while the remainder are our body language (55 percent) and voice sound (30 percent). Here, letting go of working so hard to decipher body language clues is the concession to concentrate. Don't get too critical or serious. Relax and live flexible. Be relaxed, lie back, and just lookout.

1.   **Pay attention to presentation:** While making what people notice: Do they wear a business suit and polished shoes, suited for performance, reflecting ambition? Jeans and a T-shirt, expressing ease in being casual? Strong cleavage center, a seductive choice? A pendant like a crucifix, or a Buddha that shows spiritual values?

2.   **Note Pose:** When you read the attitude of men, ask yourself: Do they keep their head up, confident? And are they driving indecisively and cowering, a symbol of poor self-esteem? Were they swaggering with a puffed-out face, a display of tremendous ego?

3.   **Track Body Movements:** • Leaning and Distance — Notice when people move. Typically speaking, we move towards what we want and away from the ones we don't.

• Arms and legs crossed — this posture indicates defensiveness, indignation, or self-defense. We prefer to aim the toes of the top leg towards the individual we are more relaxed with as they cross their legs.

• Hiding one's hands — when people put their hands on their arms, coats, or concealed things behind their back, it means they're hiding.

• Lip biting or cuticle picking — When people bite or chew their lips or pick their cuticles, they attempt to soothe themselves under strain or in an uncomfortable situation.

4. Interpretation of facial expression: The expressions on our faces will become painted. Wide frown lines indicate anxiety or too much contemplation. Crow's feet are the grin curves of love. The lips pursed suggest rage, disdain, or bitterness. A tight jaw and the rubbing of teeth are indicators of stress.

Listen to Your Intuition:

Beyond their body language and vocabulary, you will listen in to anyone. How your core knows is intuition, not something your brain suggests. Instead of reasoning, it is nonverbal knowledge that you experience through photos. When you want someone to recognize, what matters most is who the individual is, not their exterior trappings. Intuition makes you see more to tell a deeper tale than the apparent.

Intuitive indications guide through:

1.   Honor your gut feelings: Listen to what your gut suggests, a spontaneous reflex that happens before you have a chance to reflect, particularly at first meetings. Whether you are at peace or not, it relays. Inner emotions are easy to arise, a primitive reaction. They are your internal meter of reality, relaying whether you can trust humans or not.

2.   Feel the Goosebumps: They are wonderful emotional tingles that express that we connect with others who push or encourage us or say something that strikes a chord.

3.   Pay attention to bursts of wisdom: In discussions with individuals that arrive in a snap, you can get an "ah-ha" Keep alert. You might skip it otherwise. We prefer to move straight to the next idea, and such crucial ideas are forgotten easily.

4.   Look for intuitive empathy: Often, you may sense the physical signs and feelings of others in your body, which is a type of extreme empathy. And, as people are thinking, notice: "Did my back hurt when it wasn't before? During an uneventful conference, am I discouraged or upset?" Want reviews to decide whether it is empathy.

Sense Emotional Energy:

Emotions are a beautiful representation of the energies we send off, the "vibe." Such we record with intuition. Several people are feeling happy to be around; they are enhancing your morale and stamina. Some are draining; you want to run away naturally. While intangible, this "subtle force" may be sensed inches or miles from the body. It's named chi in Chinese medicine, an energy which is important to wellbeing.

Some of the strategies to read emotional energy are:

1.   Sense for the presence of People: It is the total force we produce, not always associated with language or actions. It is the emotional aura that covers us like a storm of clouds or the light. Note as you read people: Will they have a welcoming aura that attracts you? And do you have the willies, which have you head back?

2.   Watch Eyes of People: Our eyes express strong strength. Just like the brain has an electromagnetic signal which stretches throughout the body, studies show that the eyes are also transmitting this. Allow time to observe eyes from individuals. Will they care? What's Sexy? Pleasant? Midway? Furious? Determine also: Is there anyone in their eyes at home, suggesting an affection capacity? Or do they sound guarded or hidden?

3.   Remember the essence of a Handshake, Embrace, and Touch: We exchange emotional energy like an electric current by physical interaction. Tell yourself, would an embrace or handshake feel nice, relaxed, and confident? And is it off-putting that you'd prefer to retire? Is the hands of the citizens clammy and show fear. And walk, indicating that he is non-committal and shy?

4.   Listen to the rhythm of voice and chuckle: Our speech sound and pitch will say a lot about our emotions. The wavelengths of sound produce sensations. Note how the rhythm of voice influences you while hearing others. Ask yourself: Does it sound calming in their tone? Or is it snippy, abrasive, or whiny?

How to understand people and their actions?

1. Past experiences and understanding people:

When the new-born kid goes into adulthood, he starts to establish those expectations that will lead him for the remainder of his life. For example, a child that his parents often favored could grow up as an adult needing attention to retain the attention he used to get.

A little girl who witnessed her father cheating on her mother might develop a fear of marriage, distrust of men, and even become homosexual.

So the secret to knowing the mindset of a guy is to learn about the aspirations he's working toward as a consequence of the circumstances he'd gone in throughout his life before. Any time you look at the acts of the individual from this angle, you will notice the behavior you have previously identified as odd makes all sense in the universe.

A common tomboy is a girl who plays football, who likes to wear black, and most of her mates are men. From a shallow point of view, people classify her as crazy, psycho, or weirdo, but you can quickly appreciate her behavior as you have a better picture of the circumstances she has been through. As a little child, this girl felt neglected by her father because instead of a daughter, he wanted a son. The girl started believing at this point that the girls are evil, faulty, and frail. As a consequence, because she disliked becoming frail like other people, she unintentionally formed the urge to become as powerful as a man.

2. Understanding people's superstructures:

Personality of the person is like a massive, highly intertwined, super framework. A girl may be terrified of darkness because deep inside her, she feels unstable in life as a consequence of watching her jobless dad wasting his time partying rather than protecting the family's future. Throughout this stage, the subconscious mind unintentionally tells the girl of her insecurity each time she sees herself in a dark room.

For example, a girl cannot sleep at night because people generally know she is scared of ghosts. But in reality, by reading her superstructures, the feelings of vulnerability that she felt are actually a result of losing her father a couple of months ago, and that is the one responsible for her fear of darkness, revealed.

When attempting to explain the psyche of individuals, you don't have to distinguish their acts, behavior, desires they have, and their mentality from each other as all of these aspects are either explicitly or implicitly related to each other.

3. Understanding people's psychology in a few steps:

In order to understand people's personality, you need to:

• Look deep beyond actions: Don't only check at acts, but seek to get at the reasons behind them even though the behavior sounds odd.

• Unmet needs are the secret to understanding people: Aspirations, motivations, or unmet needs that the individual discovers at an early age may be the key to understanding the individual. Make sure you look at the behavior of the individual from this angle.

• All is interconnected: If someone wants to wear nice clothing then that may be attributed to the question of his self-image that may be embedded in the rejections he had from the other sex earlier in his existence (Just as an example)

4.3 Relaxing Couples by Assigning Activities (or you can do by self-help)

Compatibility is important in romantic partnerships; however, when life's pressures seem like they're piling on you, the commitment you're putting into your spouse can fall into your periphery. It is especially valid for people who have been together for some time; it is simple to take for granted the one who's always been there for you. Therefore more and more individuals are searching for support from qualified practitioners. If you're not yet ready to see a psychiatrist, however, there are some successful pair therapy activities that you might do.

There is a definite ebb and flow, and after you have broken apart, it is necessary to reconnect. So though quality time spent on a romantic getaway will definitely do the trick, time and resources often don't afford it. It might also seem unlikely for certain busy couples — particularly those with kids — to find time for a date night. The good news is, if you have 20 minutes, 10 minutes, or you only have five, with a few tried and tested technical strategies, you and your other half will interact with each other every single day.

Partnership experts would be discussing specific tasks that they sometimes offer their clients. If you've been in a three-month or 30-year partnership, these strategies can benefit you and your partner get on the same page, and you'll be stronger than ever.

Define & Prioritize What You Want In Your Relationship:

It is crucial to define what you need and anticipate from your partnership in order to interact effectively with your spouse. Finding your time to make a chart — and getting an S.O. do the same. Each of you is writing a sequence of short sentences beginning with the word 'we,' phrased in the optimistic in the basic present-tense. (For starters, "We hug 'hello' and 'goodbye'" or "We sit down together at least three days a week for dinner.") Then, rate the lists in order of significance and measure them. The last step is to create a master list you all decide with — and hold it in a position you use every day. Write it in a good italic script, then print it on colored paper. Write and write it together, find it perfect for framing or get it written, printed, or graved.

Identify Your Partner's Positive Traits:

Another practice to list: Partners write down what the other does to make them feel nice. These can involve items like preparing dinner, squeezing your back, or calling you for daytime check-in. Following, have a peek at each other's notes and pledge over the next week to do two or three of those items. The final move, is to show joy and admiration when your loved one succeeds.

Get Closer Through Physical Connection:

A strategy that actually lets two individuals fall into harmony is a wonderful and easy practice in love is to lie down on a sofa or bed together and synchronize the breathing. With an extra layer of closeness, you should embrace each other and place your hand on your partner's back. And, you should consider spooning, and you can both sense the rhythm and movement of your companion. Five to 10 minutes of synchronized breathing helps to balance the nervous processes of all spouses and synchronize your heartbeats. It's a really calming, soothing, and bonding activity. Lovers share at least once a day a brief 60-second embrace, allowing them a minute to bond irrespective of how busy they might be.

Make (Extended) Eye Contact:

Face gazing is another means of establishing a feeling of closeness and communication with your mate. This seems disappointingly easy, but since it's such a sensitive practice, it may be incredibly challenging to perform over long amounts of time. There is a suggestion beginning with 30 seconds and working up to three to four minutes. Don't panic if you feel self-conscious, anxious, to start screaming — that is a perfectly natural response to this fresh and insecure activity. The strength of this practice resides in the idea that you center your energies solely on each other, without any obstacles or masks to hide behind. And while eye contact can be a little difficult at first, it can be quite satisfying. The feeling of seeing honestly and being noticed by your spouse is extremely strong, bonding, and personal. She continues that this can be especially empowering in comparison to the coordinated relaxation technique above.

Let Each Other Blow Off Steam:

Job, income, family problems. A ton of issues are stressing them out. Taking 10 minutes a day working things out to let out the stress — as well as reduce the amount you waste stewing. In this exercise, one essential "law" is not to bring up complaints regarding your wife or your partnership. Take turns to moan about the day, lament, and get the partner's help. The aim is to be a good listener. Don't attempt to fix the issue. Take turns to listen and be respectful and respect your companion, even though you disagree.

Practice Arguing Constructively:

Arguing is a common aspect of every friendship when thinking about disputes. The way the debate progresses does, therefore, decide whether it is beneficial or damaging to the alliance. When a hotbutton problem emerges, there is an appropriate way you might communicate with each of your opinions. The 'speaker' and 'listener' take turns. The listener will take notes and write about what their spouse said. Then the listener explains what the spouse has just said and how they might sound internally. The listener will outline to the approval of their partner. Instead, exchange positions. Keep in mind that when debating, there are certain words you can never suggest to the S.O., like "still" and "never" blanket. Remember that being compassionate is important to love your mate and your partnership in the way you do conflict.

4.4 Music therapy Activities and Tools

Mostly what we need to unwind is strong coffee and good music. Art influences every part of our lives — physical, mental, social, and behavioral.

As a treatment is an established method of managing tension and moving into a positive frame of mind.

Counseling involves attention, conversation, and understanding. It is a common approach to relax clients and make them happy in clinics, educational facilities, and other clinical settings.

Therapy is claimed by psychiatrists to boost the quality of life. From suffering to personal failure, commitment to partnership problems, music therapy is one approach that fits all.

Music therapy has five major purposes:

- Transferring one's focus from problems to remedies.
- Providing a rhythmic pattern for calming and respiration.
- Helping consumers to see happy things that elicit joy and enjoyment.
- To help them to achieve a deeply relaxed state.
- Mood varies.

Therapy remains unquestioned as a treatment for emotional emotions and strain.

What are Music Therapy Activities and Tools?

Music therapy is a treatment of the creative form. Whether you're composing a record, listening to it, or performing alongside it – music therapy needs some sort of contact and language of either manner.

Music counseling is performed mainly under observation, where the educator utilizes specific methods or other strategies to effectively execute the plan.

Musical instruments like the guitar or piano, for example, are common methods for music therapy. Any types of music therapy often include imagination, in which the psychiatrist subtly directs the person to picture himself in a fun position and performs calming music to create the correct mood for him.

The music practitioners utilize various resources and practices.

Some of them include:

A musical instrument:

Clients want to experience the music and sing along with their therapist. Getting a guitar, ukulele, piano, or harp is nice to brighten up your game. It puts around an intense feeling of happiness and functions well in music therapy for youngsters.

A speaker:

Good for group therapy, performing music on a decent mic. This provides a sense of survival and allows clients to take an interest in the process. In fact, it always lets the psychiatrist feel that he is audible to all.

A screen for visual activities:

The therapists also hold a tablet or other tools that display the picture on the projector while utilizing visual images that complement the song. In addition to holding clients involved in the process, visual aids serve as a mechanism to maximize the music's beneficial effect on our mind.

Paper and pen:

Many music professionals are holding the pen and paper to document and receive reviews. It is often used in songwriting events or sentence finishing games where customers communicate through phrases.

Music therapy's main aim is to improve one's coping abilities, which calls for a constructive paradigm change. Professionals utilize different approaches or therapeutic music exercises to reach certain expectations.

Many music therapy exercises include:

• Reading and humming poems.

• Improvising on compositions and bits of music.

• Playing an instrument.

• Apply the equipment and musical instruments.

- Album listening (with and without the auditory imagery).

- The sharing of knowledge through songs.

Three Music Therapy Techniques:

1. Drumming:

Drumming is a perfect musical device to promote light-hearted pleasure, optimistic attachment, and unhindered dedication. Scientists believe drumming exercises increase neuronal activity, which helps the body battle neurological and endo chronological disorders.

Drumming often has a good social connotation and brings people together as part of a community, in addition to enhancing body functions.

Drumming procedures are beyond laws. Clients will pick their own direction to perform the instrument; however, they wish.

Some of the immediate advantages of drumming include:

- Anger relief, pain, and anxiety relief.

- Treat persistent pain signs.

- Enhanced digestive response.

- Sensing mutual relations.

- Emotional catharsis or release of resentment and bottled-up rage.

- Offering space for introspection and selfrealization.

2. Singing:

Singing is a common method in music therapy accessible to people of all ages and experiences. It has been integrated into numerous ways and events and is still a commonly used method for music therapy. Most scientists call the brain singing the 'mega-vitamin.'

Studies have also shown that listening to music or humming along with them tends to heal weakened brain tissue. That is why music is a vital aspect of the diagnosis in Parkinson's disease, depression, or Alzheimer's.

3. Vibro-Acoustic Therapy:

Vibro-acoustic therapy or VAT is a scientific approach that combines low-frequency vibrations with slowpaced music resonances. Sound waves tend to spread beneficial energies across the body. It stimulates the body and helps it to use the mechanisms of built-in recovery to relax the mind and body.

Music Therapy Interventions:

Treatments in music therapy are generally classed as successful treatments and responsive interventions. All types of music therapy treatments typically allow the use of the influence of tunes and sound vibrations to reach the human mind to help it maintain a calm condition. Whether an individual makes music, performs it, or listens to it, the immediate emotions evoked by the cycle help to bring about the optimistic change of emphasis.

Effective music approaches are the ones that engage clients and clinicians together in the therapy phase. Ideal forms of successful music therapy treatments include events such as dance, collective singing, individual presentations, or musical playing.

Clients are often viewers rather than participants of active or inactive treatments. Such treatments include music calming therapy, mediation with relaxing songs, or the like.

Neurologic Music Therapy, or NMT, is a common music therapy that many neuroscientists focus on. This is a research method that tracks brain processes in order to cause positive improvements in the person before and during listening to soothing material. NMT is a popular treatment to assist people with neuro-linguistic problems, and it also aims to improve communication abilities in adolescents and young adults.

History of Music Therapy in Action:

A bone flute that was probably around 40,000 years ago was the first evidence of a musical instrument. Partially owing to these ancient connections between music and human life, the pervasive influence between music therapies that more or less many of us undergo.

There has been music therapy there since the Stone Age. Ancient peoples and indigenous communities such as Australia's Aborigines and certain African groups used singing and community musical practices to pray, rejoice, or pass through difficult times (such as famine, floods, or severe weather).

The Ancient Greek culture still leaves evidence of how music was introduced into their lives and felt that that was the best way to preserve the harmony of mind and body.

Musings of Plato and Pythagoras provide some examples of how the Greeks tried to help one another through music and promoted music education and understanding in their societies.

The famous example of a real-life music therapy program is in autism care. Autistic adolescents, who have diminished social and cognitive skills, react to musical stimulation more strongly than other forms of communication. This catches and sustains their interest for a longer time.

Research has also found that teaching everyday tasks to children of various skills by musical acts tends to better cement the knowledge and to internalize the information faster.

Common Questions on the Usage of Music Therapy: Before taking part in music therapy classes, several participants and carers come up with some concerns regarding the effectiveness of music therapy.

Several of the common things people ask include:

• What is music therapy?

• How does it work to boost health?

• How many days will we have to do this?

• How does it influence attitude and emotions?

• Where will we bring it to practice?

• Who will tell us all about the music therapy?

- Is music therapy and music calming essentially the same?

Some free guides and forums give us an overview of what we should learn and who we can speak to before showing up for music therapy.

How is the treatment for music, and how does it work?

What benefits does music therapy offer?

A Look at the Clinical Usage of Music Therapy (Three music therapy activities and exercises):

Music therapy work is at its height, and many popular music therapies and approaches are adapted to our interests in a special way. Here is a collection of common community music therapy events and other treatments you might want to know more.

1. Music Bingo:

Music bingo is a computational music task that stimulates awareness and attention towards reality. This is a common approach for adult treatment, which is sometimes employed to enhance emotional wellbeing in combination with other types of counseling.

The exercise includes creating cards where each person sketches a tune, and after assuming the name is right, others sing it. It can be performed as a band or in pairs, which works well for people with impaired memory abilities.

2. Music Relaxation:

Relaxation of listening is a well-known music treatment for reflection and mindfulness. Music relaxation's primary aim is to create a relaxed environment in which the subconscious can relax, and the muscles will loosen up to release the built-up tension.

Several yoga retreats, music therapy, is a crucial factor in which teachers adjust the space lighting and eliminate any potential disturbances before performing the tracks. It's always a perfect way to unwind each day, helping to develop cognitive endurance over time. This technique can be very helpful to soothe distorted partners.

3. Music Selection:

Music choice is utilized by children or people with mental and self-regulation issues. The method includes having clients pick a piece of music they learn. Self-selected musical parts elicit feelings and carry back memories that may be connected with it.

Choice is also followed by directed mental visualization where the psychiatrist encourages the person to visualize himself in a fun setting as the background music begins to play. It's a meditative activity that produces absolute consciousness and recognition of oneself. This meditative activity proved to be the best one for relaxing partners when they are being interrupted by relationship issues and helping them to have a happy married life again.

Application Ideas for Kids:

The music stimulates children's sensory perception. We know how to talk, articulate, and appreciate by listening to music and performing it.

Music therapy motivates adolescents of all ages and is an effective solution to adolescent stress treatment, impulse regulation issues, and attentionrelated disturbances.

For classrooms, private clinical services, care centers, and foster homes, instrumental therapies for children are included. The shared aim is to uplift their morale and help them better control their anxiety.

Many experts believe that the children's music therapy operates well in a social environment. Performing as part of a team lets them build peer relationships and resolve whatever depression they have been faced by.

Either in classrooms or other places, social events assist with:

- Meeting people with common challenges and building empathy.

- Communicating within the community and inspiring each other.

- To automatically communicate and respond to stimuli.

- Creating partnerships and helping each other resolve their isolation.

- Increased communication capabilities, response speeds, and preparation.

- Creating healthy and self-confident coping strategies.

The participation of families and instructors in children's music therapy is indeed an ideal way to restore the connections they have with their parents. Musical activities enable them to feel closer to each other and seek pleasure while sharing time with each other without disruptions.

Two Music Therapy Worksheets:

Using Music to Express Feelings:

Music therapy involves catharsis of the feelings and self-expression. The worksheet 'Use Music to Share Emotions' allows clients through such artistic gestures to speak up to their innermost feelings.

The exercise is easy, which involves the measures that follow. This is arbitrary and self-storable, and in reality, there are no correct or wrong responses. Here is a short summary of the worksheet, and the Positive Psychology toolkit provides you with more detail.

Instructions – Select three songs that you believe reflect your current circumstance and feelings. Address the following questions about each of the songs you've picked and remain truthful to yourself. Recall that here, there are no correct or wrong responses.

1. Which are the Track titles?

2. When you hear the songs, what comes to your mind?

3. How do they make you feel?

4. Which is the important part of the track to you, and why?

Draw What You Hear Worksheet:

This worksheet is used for both human and community purposes in a variety of environments. The function is basic and requires actions such as:

1.   At the start of the interview, clients assess their listening abilities.

2.   The psychiatrist then introduces them to a few pieces of material, telling them to listen to each other properly.

3.   Each individual receives a worksheet at the next stage, where they can compose, draw, or report what they feel after listening to the pieces of music.

These two Music therapy worksheets play a significant role in restoring the couple's relations by making each one of them relax and calm. Through this method, each person can easily asses his or her weakness and then works for it to overcome. This method can be categorized as a self-analysis technique for identifying problem creating actions.

A Take-Home Message:

Music reduces stress and brings us back to ourselves. It is one of the strongest ways to overcome depression and isolation, and also provides us with the courage to confront and convey the intense feelings that drive much of our acts.

Using music as a tool for calming, human, or collective action may produce beneficial improvements in the working of the heart, blood pressure rates, and overall body functions. May you're an active listener or an active participant, music will change your life for the better in every way.

4.5 Art therapy Techniques for De-stressing

Art therapy is a type of therapy focused on the idea that constructive creativity will aid us in recovery, self-esteem, or just chilled out. It's unusual in that most other types of counseling depend on language as the main means of communication, whereas painting needs something more, something more complicated to describe.

Look at 15 methods in art therapy to make you calm and feel de-stressed:

1. Design a postcard that you don't intend to send:

If it's a romantic note to somebody you're not ready to admit your emotions yet, or an agitated outburst you realize is better kept unsaid, enumerating all the information also helps deflate the matter at hand. Although writing the text may be soothing in its own way, the postcard design gives the material much more meaning. This also helps you to stimulate different parts of your brain when relaxing in a coloring book-like way. When you throw the signed and sealed letter into the garbage (or tuck it safely in a drawer), you'll find that some of the influence has been lost.

2. Cut and paste a painting to make a collage:

Create a drawing on paper or cardboard stuff. When you're finished, trim or take it down. Using the bits instead as building blocks for a new work of art — a collage. See how the first artwork is something fresh and interesting, something unforeseeable. This practice illuminates the near connection between creation and disaster and inspires one to take chances of actively challenging oneself and certain facets of life.

3. Build an altar to a loved one:

Take inspiration from a type of art known as folk art and create an altar that celebrates a special partnership, living or not, between you and someone else. Decorate the shrine with portraits, letters, and artifacts of happy times spent together, as well as new works of art that you have produced in their memory. From the presents you've shared with a candy wrapper that you know your topic would enjoy, everything can become creative stuff. Creating another person's totem awakens memories and provides a tangible representation of a connection that can offer relief in challenging times.

4. Draw in total darkness:

So much of the stress that we experience when making art comes from the judgments and the criticism that every step of the way seems inevitable. In complete darkness, seek to build artwork to liberate art from the art critic within your mind. Think of it as a way of drawing on blind contours. Immediately you are liberated to build curves, forms, and patterns only because you feel like you should. Once you switch the lights off, we believe that what you see would shock you.

5. Watercolor your bodily state:

Lie down flat, and cover your door. Visualize the body while breathing in and out. Seek and picture a certain color of your air when it leaves your mouth, another color as it exists. What are you watching? Draw a body outline on a wide sheet of paper and build an aquarelle inside, depending on your body state. Think of all these colors, where they are densest, where they are more invisible, say to you. Find this the most soothing self-portrait you're ever going to make.

6. Create a Zentangle-inspired creation:

It is a style of drawing developed by Rick Roberts and Maria Thomas to make drawing meditative and open to everyone. You have to be instructed by a Zentangle Instructor to understand the approved process so you can replicate the simple concept on your own. Using a sheet of parchment, cut into a rectangle of the 3.5-inch square and draw a freehand border in light pencil along the bottom of it. Then use a pencil to draw a curved line or squiggle within the boundary, named "loop." Now turn to a pen and start drawing a "tangle," a set of patterns and shapes around your "net" and voila. You have a Zentangle to yourself. The method is structured to promote deliberate, ceremonial formation and make space for human error — no erasing, that's against the law. Traditional Zentangles are usually black and white, but we embrace complete color exploration. It shouldn't take the whole cycle longer than 15 minutes and can be replicated anytime you have the urge. Keep some squares handy, so when inspiration strikes, you can always create them.

7. Produce a permission slip:

Think of the day-to-day social and self-imposed stresses that you experience, the human characteristics you see as mistakes, the inevitable drops you see as errors. Pick one of these things, and grant yourself permission to do just that in ornamental detail. Turning one easy loss into a success will reduce self-hatred emotions, allowing you to meet more of your main goals. Note, this is an art project, so render it perfect.

8. Write a found poem:

You do not dream of yourself as a poet? Let anyone else do the hard part of picking the content from old books, journals, newspapers, or even letters to come up with the terms. Break words in, or encourage you to leap back. Collage the found materials just like a visual collage you would. In the outset, you may have a subject or tale in mind, or just get going and see where the word collaging takes you.

9. Craft a mark-making tool unique to you:

Instead of wasting much of your time on a real painting, why not concentrate a little of the energy on creating an all your own substitute paintbrush? Either it's a row of some toothpicks glued to a cardboard base and dipped in paint or a DIY paintbrush made from pom-poms and yarn; you can make a mark-making tool out of just about anything. After actually creating a piece of your latest device, you'll have relinquished some of your creative influence to your distinct artistic medium, which is a work of art in itself, of course.

10. Make a forgiveness box:

If there's a particular person — including yourself — you don't want to harbor any more negative emotions, try to make him or her a box of forgiveness. Decorate a small box with some nice images and words that can either be individualspecific or cater to your desired inner state. You can write the name of an individual on a paper slip, and if you prefer, insert it in the box, and the name can be removed and exchanged if necessary. The process of making the box will bring forth happy memories of whomever the box is for, as well as help you to work physically toward a place of pardon.

11. Create a color collage:

Color has the ability to affect our moods. However, often, instead of utilizing color to change our present state of mind, it is good to take a moment and dig deeper into the color that you are feeling today. Feeling uninhibited and hot-tempered? Cut and paste orange pictures to suit your mood. Living inside your own emotional condition will make you appreciate why you act the way you do and know that it might not be such a terrible place to be.

12. Make a power mask:

Very frequently we think of wearing a mask as a means of concealing things about ourselves, but often this veil of security and secrecy allows us to feel free and really helps to convey things genuine, complicated, and honest. Build a strength mask packed with icons that make you feel confident (think of the outfit of an actress, or the helmet of an athlete). If you brace for a tough scenario — whether it's dinner with the immediate family or a speech at work — you should strap it on to show to yourself that you can perform the job with or without the mask.

13. Construct a holiday "anti-calendar":

Far too frequently, schedules are jam-packed with tasks, obligations, and commitments, rendering the coming days more a source of tension than ease. Seek to build a DIY Advent Calendar that we called an anti-calendar. Rather than sending yourself a cookie every day, treat yourself to a smile, a doodle, an inspirational quotation, or an empowering order like "eat breakfast every day in bed." When anything goes according to schedule, you could find yourself jumping out of bed every morning like a child on Christmas day.

14. Start a doodle chain:

A doodle's unlikely to appear evil. You may find it extremely hard to quit drawing until you give in to the infinite possibilities that exist when the wiggly line reaches an unidentified shape. Begin with a friend or loved one, a doodle-centric take on an exquisite corpse to loosen your connection to your creation. Watching your single squiggle blossom into a spindly beast in front of your eyes is pretty amazing. You should even test that out with a penpal on chain mail for a more positive twist.

15. Draft a portrait of a past self:

We are not thinking about previous lives, just parts of yourself that you feel like maybe you've lost contact with or outgrown. If you are revisiting a time of confusion, denial, or just plain different, use the gap between recollection and imagination as your focus helps to illustrate how malevolent yourself really is. It looks, for the first time in years, like reading your old journal.

Actually tells about a person's vision of mind like how he or she sees things, persons, and matters. So by having tiny techniques of art therapy, a distorted partnership can work out again. As each person can get the opportunity to analyze the problem creating areas of the other partner as well as of his, her own.

Chapter 5: Deepening Connections and Bonds

The major approach of this chapter is how to deepen connections and bonds between partners. How to care about each other, how to maintain a strong relationship and keep it in balance is all discussed in detail.

5.1 Emotional Connection

An emotional link is the bond that unites people. It is the adhesive in the relationships. Most couples do not know that the bond that holds them together weakens if they don't frequently interact on an emotional level.

Something occurs to our minds when we feel separated physically from a companion or family. We may feel that our sense of protection is being undermined, rendering us afraid. The amygdala, the almond-shaped midbrain area, functions as a warning device, and a feeling of fear will set in.

If we don't get comfort from reconnecting with loved ones, that will place us in a mental condition of hyper aroused. It, in effect, will induce elevated cortisol to raise our stress rates. Physical and mental health and wellbeing can decline if cortisol remains elevated for a long period of time.

It is a study that happy and emotionally wise people do exercise: shifting toward one another. Turning toward is a subtle or quick constructive interaction that can intensify an emotional bond between a pair.

Once couples turn to each other, they exercise "offers." Offers are efforts to communicate with each other through love, encouragement, laughter, or interest. These can be vocal or nonverbal communication. An individual may be aware or unaware of the use of a bid, which may look like any of these following: • A gentle touch

• A hug or kiss

• A smile

• A kind remark

• Listening

• A playful gesture

• A word of encouragement

• Sharing a news event

• Saying "I love you".

Every day, one of the secrets of lasting love between couples is turning towards one another in small ways. People who frequently practice communicating emotionally remain together longer than others who won't.

Couples who don't practice daily offers will lose their way more quickly. When we don't interact consistently with each other emotionally, our loved ones can feel uncared for or unvalued. The trap of taking a spouse or companion for granted can creep up, particularly when the pair have long been together.

It's understandable, despite our active and hectic lives, how we might lose track of having a loved one realize how much we appreciate them. There's a greater risk of emotional disconnection when we feel burdened, overwhelmed, or stressed.

How to Emotionally Connect With Your Partner:

Here are two significant things you can do to emotionally connect with your partner or spouse:

1. Being intentional and exercising emotional connection every day that can make a big difference:

You don't have to wait for and schedule an extravagant holiday to link emotionally. You might start right now, wherever you are.

Here are given a few ideas to get you on the move. When you're next to your companion or partner, seek and reach out to grab their side. When you're not with your companion or spouse, write or call a nice note to let them know you're worried about them.

When you practice communicating emotionally every day, it's like bringing capital into your mental bank account. You participate more in the partnership. The more you bring your love in, the more growth it will develop. In tough times maintaining a large savings plan will benefit.

2.   Enlist the things you can do to lean in toward your partner:

If that sounds simple, it is. List the things you can do to turn your partner around. It can be a mind or a written list. This could take a little bit of time and effort, especially if you got out of practice. Putting the list in a position you will see frequently can make you continue to reach out and communicate.

Follow this experiment for a month to see if the interpersonal link will continue to reshape to build a stronger relationship. Consistency is key; the higher the number, the better the relationship will be.

5.2 Relationship Therapy: Enhancing Romantic Relationships

Throughout today's society, it can appear nearly difficult to establish or sustain a safe and stable partnership.

With all the additional pressures of living in the modern era, the omnipresent interruptions of social networking, and the breakneck speed our lives are now undergoing, maintaining a healthy partnership with your partner or loved one-sound like a herculean job.

Although no partnership is made up entirely of sunshine and flowers, a stable, optimistic, and mutually advantageous partnership is not impossible to enjoy. This can involve some effort from both parties, but the secret to achievement is in your hands.

Whether you and your significant other struggles to make time for each other, finding it hard to communicate effectively, or dealing with something a little heavier than the average stressors of modern relationships, relationship therapy (also known as relationship counseling, couple counseling, and couple therapy) can be an important key to success in relationships.

How Relationship Therapy Can Help:

There are several various forms of treatment that may be used in marriages, but all of them share the same goal: strengthening or increasing the partnership.

In general, the phrase "partnership therapy (or counseling)" applies to intimate relationship therapy with adolescents, but there are definitely many partnerships that treatment will gain from.

The essence of human contact naturally contributes to certain discord, conflicts, or issues between individuals. In long-term intimate partnerships, including marriage, this inherent inclination is exacerbated. The more time we invest with others, increasing the probability that we will ultimately encounter an obstacle that endangers the partnership.

While couples are expected to sometimes disagree, or even engage in (non-physical) fights, there is a fine line between normal relationship stress and more serious issues.

A partnership or marriage therapist may assist a person dealing with all these problems, whether their support is in the form of educating clients regarding healthy conflicts and battling safe, or finding and resolving things that deeply affect the partnership.

The aims of the counseling process of each person, and also of each group, that vary based on the issues they contend with, but there are five basic concepts that govern the counseling in relationships.

The aim of relation therapy is to:

Change the couple's views on the relationship:

We also get wrapped up in old conduct habits or thinking processes, which may help us lose sight of the bigger picture. When it comes to how we react to the issues in the relationship, we could have a blind spot by focused on what our spouse is "doing wrong."

Marital therapy can help the pair step back and have a more realistic perspective of the partnership in general, as well as the particular difficulties they are facing. The pair should be motivated to avoid worrying about the guilt and continue acting as a team to solve their issues together.

Modify any dysfunctional behavior:

Perhaps one of the intimacy therapist's most significant tasks is to help people improve their actions towards each other, especially the possibly negative behaviors. Only someone with the highest intentions will unintentionally inflict undue discomfort or injury to their spouse, whether it be physical, psychological, or emotional hurt.

The psychiatrist should approach certain patterns and direct the cycle of identifying, accepting, and modifying them to his or her clients. Such activities can vary from poor contact patterns to physical aggression whenever possible. The psychiatrist may prescribe that the pair spend time apart in serious situations, or that either or more people undergo additional care or counseling for a particular problem such as drug abuse.

Decrease emotional avoidance:

Communication is the foundation of an interaction, whether by spoken words, sign language, text messages, or emails or body language. Both partners must express their emotions with each other for a friendship to thrive. Although we each have our own degree of ease in expressing personal thoughts and emotions, there is a certain standard of contact that must exist for a stable partnership to be feasible.

A relationship therapist may help the couple convey emotions they may be reluctant to communicate with each other, or first felt awkward communicating. Anxiety prevents successful contact, and the psychiatrist should meet with the pair to help relieve the concerns that accompany their exchange of feelings.

Improve communication:

Communication is essential to the reparation and restoration of friendly ties. Apart from empowering couples to exchange feelings with each other, couples do need to know how to interact constructively with each other in general.

The therapist can mentor the clients to develop their communication skills in addition to educating the pair about good contact and pitfalls to avoid while communicating with each other. The emphasis here is not just on interacting efficiently but also on caring, which involves active listening and empathy.

Promote strengths:

A supportive counselor or psychiatrist who uses positive psychological methods would certainly rely more on this theory than other practitioners, although to a degree, all interpersonal counseling would focus on this. Each partnership has its strengths and weaknesses, and while much counseling may concentrate on the flaws, successful counseling often emphasizes and reinforces the strengths of the partnership.

A successful relationship therapist can help people recognize their similarities, which also encourage the clients to determine for themselves what's best for their partnership. Taking advantage of the abilities may mean more often participating in similar activities, improving their general perception of the partnership, or actually trying to focus more on the good facets of the partnership than on the negative ones.

Focusing on these five values will offer clients the resources they need to meet the difficulties of their partnership together, and come out better than ever on the other side of those difficulties.

What Romantic Relationship Theory Works for You:

The varieties of intimacy therapy are complex, illustrating the various specific partnership hypotheses that can be identified in the literature. Although the aforementioned five concepts are the core foundation blocks of relational counseling, there are other avenues to bring them into action.

Many relation hypotheses supplement or reinforce current theories, whereas others contend in partnership analysis to clarify typical patterns or unique results.

Below are some of the most widely referenced relationship theories that are explored. Such ideas cannot be deemed a thorough summary of the topic, but they also offer a solid basis in the psychology of relationships.

Social Exchange Theory:

The Social Exchange Theory of Relationships is one of the most influential ideas of partnership psychology.

The hypothesis is focused on the premise that all partnerships (including non-romantic relationships) are centered on mutual interactions or "giving and taking". This trade method, mirroring some of the fundamental ideas of economics, politics, and even philosophy, seeks to optimize the advantages of the partnership and reduce the costs that follow it.

Unlike the balancing of costs and rewards that corporate owners and CEOs participate in while evaluating their choices, the principle of social exchange implies that when deciding whether to start or maintain their partnerships, individuals use that same strategy. They leave the partnership if they consider that the risks outweigh the rewards.

The method, however, is not focused entirely on the interactions between two men. There are three main components that affect our judgments regarding relationships:

1. The correlation between what we bring into a partnership (what we give) and what we get out of the partnership (what we take)

2. The type of friendship that we feel needs

3. Chances of a better relationship with another.

Such three aspects affect how we feel regarding our partnerships and how we think about them while deciding how to start, put more time and energy into, or give up on a relationship.

We establish a measure of distinction using such criteria – a criterion that we keep for the ratio of giving and taking in a partnership. Various forms of partnerships are likely to involve varying rates of contrast – for example, you might like an approximately equivalent ratio of sharing and receiving in a marital partnership, whereas the sum you're able to offer to a kid or somebody you're mentoring would be much more lenient to you.

This analogy is a critical aspect of deciding how to do in our partnerships, but how we view the environment and people in general influences the choices we make. When we assume the universe is full of nice, fascinating, and happy individuals, we would be more inclined to break a partnership with a strong give/take ratio, while if we don't think we will find a better partnership quickly, we may put up with such a ratio.

This principle is valuable to clarify and forecast the nature of partnerships, but it does not address all the basics. Many people may consider that the kinship of social exchange theory to economics and political science is too "mathematical" and ignores some of the more complex, relational elements of relationships.

Attachment Theory:

This famous idea in relationship psychology implies that the connections that we develop first in life are the most significant influences that affect our relationships during life.

The theory of attachment is based on the study of John Bowlby, a psychoanalyst who studied the circumstances of removing children from their parents. He theorized that the intense actions children would exhibit (crying, weeping, grasping, etc.) in order to avoid breakup or reconnection with a physically separated parent were in reality survival processes, behaviors that were sharpened over centuries to guarantee the parent or parent's safety and treatment would continue.

Such attachment patterns are normal responses to the possibility of the primary caregiver sacrificing certain survival benefits. Because the children who participated in these habits were more likely to thrive, over time, the impulses were instinctively preferred and reinforced.

Such activities make up what called an "attachment behavioral system," the network that controls us in our attitudes and practices of partnership forming and preservation.

This attachment theory work has shown that children put in a strange situation (involving the breakup and reunification of parents and infants) usually respond in one of three forms:

1.   Secure attachment – these children displayed discomfort after separation but found relief when the parent(s) returned and were quickly comforted.

2.   Anxious-resistant attachment – a lower proportion of children reported higher rates of anxiety and, after

reuniting with the parent(s), tended both to pursue consolation and to attempt and "punish" the parent(s) for leaving.

3. Avoiding attachment-the third type of attachment form displayed no stress or limited stress after separation from the parent(s) and either neglected the parent(s) after reunification or deliberately resisted the parent(s).

It is apparent that such types of attachment are primarily a result of having caregiving children in their early years; those that have earned help and affection from their parents are likely to be healthy, whereas those who have encountered confusion or neglect from their parents are likely to have more concern towards their connection with their parents.

Moreover, adult attachment theory goes a step further: According to this theory, the relationships we develop as adults (especially romantic relationships) are often directly linked to our attachment styles as children and the support we receive from our parents.

The types of adult attachment that fit the same general trend mentioned above:

• Secure attachment – those adults are more likely to be content with their marriages, feel safe and linked to their spouse without having the need to be together (physically) all the time; Honesty, encouragement, freedom, and strong emotional ties possibly feature in their relationships.

• Anxious preoccupied attachment – those who develop less stable relations with their spouses that feel desperate for love or attention and believe that their spouse needs to "full" them or fix their issues. While in their romantic relationships, they long for safety and security, they may also act in ways that push away their partner, rather than invite them in. The interpersonal representations of their worries may be clingy, aggressive, angry, or quickly distracted by minor problems.

• Dismissive avoidant attachment – one of the two styles of adult avoidant attachment, typically holding those with this relationship form apart from others. They may believe they require no human contact to live or succeed and rely on preserving their freedom and alienation from others. Such individuals are also likely to mentally "wind-down" anytime a possibly hurtful situation occurs, such as a significant conflict with their spouse or a challenge to the future of their partnership.

• Fearful avoidant attachment – the second form of adult avoidant attachment is ambivalent rather than isolation. People with this type of relationship typically tend to hide their emotions, as they can quickly get frustrated. They can suffer from erratic or sudden mood changes, and risk from a romantic partner being injured. At the same time, these individuals are attracted to a spouse or future partner and are scared to near. This style finds it naturally challenging to shape and sustain positive, stable relationships with others.

This principle offers an insightful and powerful reason why we are behaving the way we are in our interactions with adults. For example, the interactions we share with our parents are not the sole aspect that affects our interactions with others, but it is obvious that they have a significant part in how we respond to others as individuals.

Triangular Theory of Love:

The Triangular Theory of Love argues that all intimate partnerships have three components. Such components can differ in degree, but each one is present in a romantic partnership to some extent.

The three constituent parts are:

1. Intimacy-feelings of closeness and interaction with our partner, which decide the relationship's "warmth."

2. Passion – the component that often drives us to pursue romantic relationships, manifesting like romance, attraction to each other, excitement, and sexual activity.

3. Decision/Commitment – The final aspect includes the choice to initiate a romantic relationship and then to pursue the relationship; this factor is what determines actions linked to continuing a relationship or terminating a relationship.

Such elements are not separated from each other; they may communicate and affect one another, rendering the resultant interaction less of a quantitative issue and more of an art form. For example, a high degree of initial excitement can cause the urge to become more familiar with your spouse, whereas increased intimacy may influence the level of commitment in a marital partnership.

The various variations of all three components manifest in eight distinct kinds of love:

- Non love – lack of all three components
- Liking – only affection, no passion or decision/commitment
- Infatuated love – just attraction, no affection or decision/commitment
- Blank love – just decision/commitment, no intimacy or attraction
- Romantic love – the existence of intimacy and excitement, no decision/commitment.
- Companion love – the presence of intimacy and determination/commitment, no passion
- Fatuous love – the presence of passion and decision/commitment, no intimacy
- Consummation or complete love – the presence of all three components.

Consummate love is the sort of partnership that most of us wish for, where we expose in our intimate relationship in the midst of romantic partnership, desire, and devotion. Companionate love is a growing kind of love felt by older partners who are willing to calculate their relationship together by the decade rather than a year. Infatuated love is the sort of love that we sometimes experience at the outset of a new relationship, characterized by a raging desire for our new spouse, but without the warmth and dedication that only time spent together will offer.

It is also common to move in a single relation between these types of love. The relationship can begin as liking, move into infatuated love, grow into romantic love, thrive in consummate love, and drift into companionate love as the relationship age increases.

Although "normal" aspects of these eight styles of relationships are uncommon, they offer a valuable structure for exploring and differentiating various kinds of love between them.

What Struggles Are You Facing?
Regardless of which romantic partnership theory you adhere to, here are several explanations why a couple may be finding support in sustaining or restoring their partnership.

Such reasons include:

- Communicating issues, if the issue is too little contact, incoherent contact, or derogatory communication.

- Premarital therapy, where partners utilize their time and resources to build a strong base before marriage.

- Sexual problems can in one or both spouses may trigger irritation, indignation, humiliation, guilt, dissatisfaction, and/or anxiety.

- Infidelity or unfaithfulness, leading to physical abuse, moral offense, or both.

- Help with handling certain partnerships that may adversely impact the marital partnership.

- Non-traditional relationships, such as polyamorous or asexual relationships, which may raise other issues besides those commonly found in traditional romantic relationships.

- Blended communities, because households of stepparents and/or step-siblings are frequently met of particular obstacles.

- Ending of a partnership, like a divorce or a partner's death, taking with it a particular range of feelings such as sorrow, rage, and sadness.

- Digital-age problems or concerns are emerging from new media, like feeling neglected, feeling bad in oneself or your partner's digital relationships, and the drawbacks in telephone, text, and tweet contact.

- Trust issues, concerns that also form a significant part of the tension of the partnership and may contribute explicitly or indirectly to even other difficulties in the road.

The list is not a comprehensive compilation of causes that could contribute to therapy for a person, but it addresses some of the more popular problems that carry clients to a professional psychiatrist.

What to Expect in Relationship Therapy:
Depending on the specific issues that clients are seeking assistance in addressing, in their sessions, therapists employ many different techniques, exercises, and tools; however, there are a set of questions and activities that you will likely find in any therapy relationship experience.

A basic outline of what you can expect from the treatment of relationships is as follows:

1.   Questions – about you, your partner, your personal stories, your relationship as a couple, and your history.

2.   Difficult discussions – it's never easy to discuss your issues, especially when you are discussing your issues in the same room with the other person.

3.   Discussion of progression of therapy – be prepared to talk about how therapy helps, hurts, or doesn't change one thing in each session; therapy is different for each couple, but a common theme in therapy is discussing how therapy itself progresses.

In couple therapy, these three components are virtually universal. It will also take a time of filling in the psychiatrist on what's going on in the partnership, explaining the issues the pair has, and addressing whether counseling is moving or not.

Interventions and Exercises in Relationship Therapy:

You will also be exposed to more specific questions, theories, exercises, and discussions, depending on the type of therapy or counseling you pursue.

Here are given some of the most common approaches and strategies for coping with issues in intimate relationships.

Showing Appreciation:

This exercise can sound too simple and simplistic. Sure this is an easy activity, but do not neglect the ability to express gratitude.

The pair should take turns guiding the practice, ensuring each partner gets their gratitude to both languages and feeling the praise of their spouse.

Start by approaching each other and making sure eye contact is established. The first partner begins by explaining one thing he or she likes and appreciates about their mate.

 Let's assume the examples; the first partner could claim, "I love doing the dishes because I hate making dishes! "Or "I love her sense of humor – she will still make me laugh at words with a prank or a dumb play." The second partner then participates in mirroring (that is, represents the gratitude of the first partner). In the examples mentioned above, that would be to mean something like "Do you really want I do the dishes at home?" And "You just like my sense of humor, even though I'm making dumb puns?" When the second partner expresses the gratitude, the first partner describes what the behavior or attribute they listed implies to them with the expression" This is so special to me because...

For instance, the partner who appreciates that he cleans after meals may claim," That is so special to me as it makes me feel valued and cared for when you take the pressure off my hands."

Not only does this simple exercise empower partners to recognize and express what they enjoy about each other, but it also presents them with an opportunity to learn about what they admire, both personally and as a group. It can help them find different ways to connect more closely or strengthen the positive aspects of their partnership. There are several possible beneficial effects, and this activity poses practically no dangers.

The Miracle Question:

The Miracle Question -an old standby for many different therapy types. This topic can be seen in both adult counseling and pair counseling, which can be extended to a wide variety of conditions, issues, or challenges.

The basic purpose of this approach is both to help the person (or couple) clarify their wishes or expectations, and to make the therapist recognize more what his or her client(s) wants to accomplish through counseling. It's particularly important for anyone who never really took the time out of their partnership to explain what they desire, either for themselves or for their spouses.

This problem can usually be posed as such:

"Suppose a miracle occurred this evening when you were asleep. Which will be some of the stuff that you would find when you woke up tomorrow that would convince you life has instantly become better?"

And though either or both clients present a situation that is completely difficult to accomplish, they may also use their reaction to explain their priorities. The psychiatrist should delve further into the "miracle" of the pair in the case of an unlikely potential future situation, by saying, "Why does it create a difference?"

This query allows the pair to dream for themselves about a more prosperous world, a world in which their challenges are solved. This exercise can contribute to increased encouragement to work towards improving their relationship, increased trust in the effectiveness of couple counseling, and also immediate (but incremental) change in interactions between the two people.

Our Shared Qualities:

Reminding the few items they have in common will also bring a lift in their feelings for each other, and a stronger confidence in their abilities to sort through their problems. This worksheet provides an opportunity to remember what makes them a great couple, and what makes it worth the effort to rebuild, reignite, or improve their relationship.

The Worksheet on Similar Attributes instructs the pair to fill up eight parts of at least three items they have in common. Completing this worksheet together, the pair should explore and recall as they move their way through the pages, or individually, with time at the end to evaluate their answers and notice the similarities and disparities.

The eight parts are as follows:

• We'd like to meet.

• Films, movies, or songs that we enjoy.

• We have fun while we.

• As partners, we're fantastic at.

- As partners, our shortcomings are.

- Special qualities that we share in common.

- Qualities that we admire in an individual.

- Three objectives for our future.

In addition to encouraging constructive dialogue and recognition of the good facets of their partnership, this worksheet gives partners an opportunity to recognize their achievements and shortcomings as a team and prepare for their mutual future. As stated earlier, identifying and encouraging the good in a partnership, and acknowledging and resolving the negative is important.

The creation or explanation of goals for the future is often a critical component of couple counseling. It is necessary to determine if the two parties are on the same page in terms of their short- and long-term priorities and, if not, to resolve the problems implicit in operating against opposite objectives. If a couple is coping with any stressors in their daily relationships or grappling with a big issue completing this worksheet is a helpful way to encourage them to reflect and speak about their partnership and explore whether they're going on.

How You Can Help Your Relationship:

Although inter partner relationship therapy is prescribed for more severe issues, counseling might not always be needed. Couples should do several activities at home to strengthen their partnership and fix any of the problems that occur in a typical partnership.

These 12 suggestions describe some of the most important measures you should take to strengthen the basis on which your partnership is built and enhance your capacity to manage and succeed as a couple:

• Take stock of what truly counts in your life. This will help you appreciate and manage your own objectives and expectations.

• Consider the solution and accept the disagreements that exist. Each pair must have at least a few stubborn disagreements; as they may yet do learn to recognize the discrepancies between them, it is important that couples reconcile.

• Define the problems, then isolate them. Although your partner might be incredibly successful at clicking one of your buttons once in a while, learn to recognize when you are genuinely upset with your partner and when you unnecessarily put your grievances at the doorstep of your partner.

• Stir up your spouse doing something right. Instead of just looking for an error or failure to capture your partner, consider "watching" your partner performing something you enjoy, respect, or appreciate.

• Treat your companion with patience. Try to surprise your partner with a thoughtful gesture or an unprompted kindness on the flipside; try not to take it on your own if your partner doesn't notice or appreciate your gesture as much as you expect.

• Cut away the partner's "couple moment." You still like doing something together, so it doesn't hurt to schedule some quality time together and do something that your spouse loves, even though it isn't your favorite sport.

• Count to ten before reacting angrily. For a cause, this popular piece of advice is still around-it's a classic. Seek to calm off or thought it through for at least ten seconds before responding to what the companion did, said, or didn't do or say.

• Discuss an unusual forum for discussing controversial topics. This may sound like a strange piece of advice, but sometimes a shift in physical location can also cause a shift in thinking – you may find creative new solutions to your problems.

• Taking the time off. Time-out is no longer solely for adolescents – it may be a nice relief if the companion has the conversation worked up. Take a moment to cool down.

• If you learn you made an error, please excuse yourself. This piece of advice couldn't be stressed sufficiently – accept it anytime you make an error, correct it where you can, and prepare to stop doing one in the future.

• Include assistance and secondary approaches. Our companion sometimes simply needs us to listen, empathize, and provide help or encouragement instead of a five-step strategy to address our problems. It is a perfect lead-in for the final bit of guidance.

• Talk closely to the companion. Looking into the eyes of your spouse and nodding along is not enough – successful partnerships involve constructive or intense listening, a process in which you listen with complete focus rather than preparing your answer, and allow your spouse to continue communicating with you before they are completely out of the way.

Take the last element, if you just take one bit of advice from all of these. Too many things come about because we don't interact easily or adequately. Successful communication is a perfect opportunity to know more about your mate, express them your respect, and keep an eye out for issues in the partnership.

Chapter 6: Psychodynamic Upgrades

A psychodynamic therapy, when it is used, and how it actually works, are all the major concerns of this chapter. It will provide you a complete understanding of psychodynamic school of thought in helping and healing couples. This chapter focuses on all the hidden issues, fears and desires of individuals, their root causes and how to get rid of them. The understanding of the concept of projective identification in psychodynamics upgrades is also given in detail. You will also get to know why and how to focus on acceptance and forgiveness for maintaining healthy commitments.

Psychodynamic Therapy

Psychodynamic therapy approaches psychoanalytic therapy in that it is an in-depth type of talk therapy focused on psychoanalytic ideas and concepts. Yet psychodynamic counseling is less concentrated on the interaction between counselor and psychiatrist, as it is more concentrated on the interaction between the individual and his or her outside environment. Psychodynamic treatment is generally quicker in terms of duration and amount of sessions than psychoanalytic counseling, although this is not necessarily the case.

When It's Used

Psychodynamic counseling is used mainly in the diagnosis of depression and other severe psychological problems, particularly those that have lost sensation in their life and have trouble in establishing or sustaining intimate ties. Research also has shown other successful psychodynamic treatment uses include depression, social anxiety disorder, and eating disorders.

What to Expect

The patient is allowed to speak openly, with the aid of the psychiatrist, about everything that comes to mind, including current problems, worries, wishes, visions, and fantasies. The aim is to achieve a reversal of symptoms but also to reap advantages such as improved self-esteem, greater utilization of their own strengths and skills, and an expanded capacity to establish and sustain more fulfilling partnerships. Once counseling has concluded, the individual can undergo continued changes. While for certain people, short-term therapy of one year or less may be appropriate, long-term therapy might be essential for others to achieve permanent benefits.

How It Works

The ideas and methods that differentiate psychodynamic treatment from other counseling forms provide an emphasis on identifying, accepting, knowing, communicating, and resolving unpleasant and conflicting thoughts and repressed emotions to strengthen the emotional interactions and relationships of the individual. It involves having the individual realize how repressed earlier feelings have an effect on present decision-making, actions, and interactions. Psychodynamic counseling also seeks to support people who are mindful of the roots of their psychological challenges but are powerless to solve their own issues. Through this thorough study and examination of previous interactions and feelings, people begin to evaluate and overcome their existing challenges and modify their actions in current relationships.

Looking for in a Psychodynamic Therapist

A psychodynamic practitioner is a trained, skilled social worker, psychotherapist, or other psychiatric or behavioral health specialists with specialized psychoanalysis training. Search for a psychodynamic practitioner with whom you feel confident sharing personal problems, in addition to seeking someone with the correct professional history and applicable expertise.

6.1 Focusing on Hidden Issues, Fears, and Desires
Hidden Fears and Relationship

Often couples pass their everyday lives harboring latent doubts and inhibitions within them. Partners can keep their hidden anxieties from each other, their families, and the world. Many couples struggle with the worry of revealing their secret anxiety inside a partnership. And for many couples, the responsibility of confidentiality comes at a high price for marriages that are responsive, caring, and trustworthy.

Maybe your secret fear derives from childhood; fear of the dark; fear of confidence; fear of shame; fear of inadequacy and inferiority; fear of identity; fear of social commitment; fear of intimacy; fear of becoming who you really are in life? Is the insecurity may be a family secret? Was it a perception of disease; of psychiatric illness; of phobia? Maybe you're still scared to speak about your concerns with the person nearest to you, your partner? Maybe you think thinking about your worries just makes them worse? Perhaps you feel like thinking about your anxieties would render you seem dumb? Maybe you fear you may lose respect for your partner? You might think: "Oh, maybe, maybe, maybe I should speak to a good friend but not my partner?"

Living every day with latent worries will drain your vitality and your sense of self-esteem and selfconfidence. Some within you ought to break loose, confess everyone, and become the true person you are. And lack of terror still keeps you off. "If only" is a futile refrain. But even as the caterpillar is waiting to come free of its cocoon, as you let go of terror, the transition into the butterfly awaits.

After all, revealed worries might not be so frightening. It will set you safe. It can dissipate the doubts that have plagued your days and overshadowed your future. Via a fresh prism of optimism and confidence, you'll begin to see human life and love ties. Perhaps rewarding of all, as you confess your worries to your friend, you can most definitely realize that he/she has indeed harbored secret concerns-all this time.

Exploring your doubts for your companion freely and candidly may be beneficial. More importantly, it will create a fresh sense of cohesion, a greater degree of belief, and restored trust inside your partnership. It will also make things simpler for your partner to discuss and express his / her worries and even encourage both of you to see each other like never before.

Fears may come back at various times of your life, or new fears can pop up. So having already called your fears, by voicing and discussing them inside your friendship, you would have learned how to handle and conquer fears. Fears have less control because you're not alone from them and single.

Exercise

Share the latent doubts you both carry with your companion. Discuss the concerns emerging inside your partnership. Commit to address your concerns when they emerge with all of you and assist each other in overcoming them.

20 Signs Someone Has Abandonment Issues and How to Overcome Them

Was the anxiety of breaking up damaging your relationships? Make no regrets; you're not lonely. Millions like you battle this self-sabotaging conviction and the habits that go with them. We should discuss each of the key indicators of problems of abandonment and help you recognize which ones relate to you. Identifying it is the first move to change every conviction. Only then will you seek counseling and do the research necessary to shift your attitude to a more favorable place. We'll explore how any of these things might lead to a partnership that doesn't work out. It is necessary because broken marriages intensify the anxiety that you have around abandonment. What are the warning flags that you should use to recognize problems of alienation inside yourself or others?

Signs of Abandonment Issues

1.   You Attach Too Quickly

When you encounter somebody, you travel in the blink of an eye from the first date to "in a relationship."

You assume if you don't do that, you risk dating them to someone else they want better. You don't allow them to be "the one that got away," but you don't offer yourself the time and emotional room available to determine how the partnership is moving. You don't ask if anyone you should spend the rest of your life with is this guy. Isn't it that, for what we are all searching for after all?

2.   You Move On Too Quickly

You don't allow yourself room to relax (and grieve) until you're on to the next after one partnership finishes. You are not concerned with the breakup's personal consequences. First, you leap head into something different and thrilling to relieve yourself from the discomfort and hurt that you experience. You're one of those people who "must" be in a relationship, and while you're single, you're a mess. Alas, you don't give yourself time to handle the split. You don't grieve the loss of your last partnership, or repair the damage it may have created.

3.   You're A Partner Pleaser

You strive to impress others at any moment in your relationships, like.

Moral expectations and a desire to go along with whatever the mate wishes are the result.

Are putting your wellbeing second to theirs? You are scared they would search elsewhere if you don't satisfy their wishes. When you start resenting having to do any of this stuff that can inevitably lead to confrontation. And this may lead you to abandon ship, assuming it won't ever work out between you two.

4.   You Stay In / Settle for Unhealthy Relationships

Instead of being lonely, you're able to live in a circumstance you realize deep down is not ideal for you.

Maybe you know the match isn't as successful as you originally assumed. And through the companion lies, cheats or otherwise becomes violent. Such issues just aren't quite enough for you to call it quits.

5.   You Look For Flaws in Your Partner

It's not just the case that the match isn't good; it's that you don't want it to be.

Breakup issues indicate you're concentrating on your partner's weaknesses. You are missing all the good qualities. This way, as things go south, at last, you will convince yourself that they were not right for you anyway. You are finding a beauty that resides nowhere other than in your mind. Sadly, the strategy would definitely lead to the partnership breakup.

6.   You're Reluctant to Fully Invest in a Relationship

Clearly you may be fast to consider a Zero to Sixty partnership, but that doesn't imply you're ready to invest in it.

In reality, you always reject something that signifies sincere involvement. Events like being together with their families, settling in together, and planning a "life" together.

Doing so, you give your spouse a warning that you do not see the partnership as important or longterm. It could mean the start of the end of things for you both.

7. You Avoid Emotional Intimacy

Perhaps it's no wonder that when you ignore any efforts, your spouse makes at emotional affection you feel reluctant to engage in a partnership. It will be showing weakness to let your guard down, so you're not prepared to face the hurt that this will bring. So you keep your guard up and make up for it in certain respects. Instead, you concentrate on sexual contact and seek to satisfy your mate, as pointed out above. The dilemma is that while you will be able to survive without this stuff, perhaps not your companion would be. Even if they aren't, they could come together to doubt the future.

8. You Feel Unworthy Of Love

The aspect that prevents you from getting involved with others is a deep-seated feeling of insignificance physically. You really cannot understand how anybody might really value you, and you never let someone tell you these three precious terms. If they ever touch the lips of a spouse, the reaction would be a fast and definitive "you don't love me," and that'll be it.

9.   You're Insecure:

There is no chance in your head that someone will ever accept you when you're unable to value yourself. The self-esteem has gone silent. Each choice you make is in question. Many issues you have worries about (not just the relationships).

And this may lead to further issues like:

10.   You're   Jealous   of   Every Friend/Colleague/Acquaintance

There is a good possibility, in your opinion, that your companion would be unfaithful. Any single friendship that the mate has is strictly platonic. Unsurprisingly, you'll concentrate all of your envy on representatives of the opposite sex. Yet you still get jealous as you spend time with same-sex mates and the pleasure that they get from it. This competitive behavior can weaken the bond. This would potentially provoke complaints and ill-feelings.

11.   You Struggle To Trust

The imagination conjures up thoughts of unfaithfulness, and you find it hard to trust a spouse to the full. Trust needs you to be honest, and we've already spoken about how you struggle to let down your guard. You say to yourself that thinking the worst is safer and being proved mistaken than the other way around. That is the pessimist that you are worried about. Unfortunately, the partner is searching to feel comfortable. You can agree with that; it's not fun to feel that somebody you respect doesn't trust you.

12.   You Get Separation Blues

You want to spend as close as possible near and around your spouse, because every time spent apart is wanted torment.

Separating yourself for a few hours or days has the potential of resurfacing your separation problems. It takes you down a vortex of uncertainty and depression, downwards.

It's actually the reverse of "out of sight, out of view." What you can do is ruminate on whom they go, for whom they go, and what they do. This can escalate to overbearing habits such as following up by text message on your spouse or calling every hour.

13.   You Visualize Your Partner Leaving You

Time separated offers the ideal mental atmosphere to succeed out the fear of loss.

Minds are joining a deep and threatening circle where you might foresee that your companion finishes things with you. You think to talk of the ensuing pain and chaos.

The body responds to these feelings as though they were real, and you are having episodes of intense anxiety and depression.

14.   You Overanalyze Things

Your mind is not one that would allow something to go unnoticed. You see and learn it, and then   get to work attempting to sort out the secret significance in all of it.

You're around; there is no such thing as a little statement or an insignificant gesture. You can take a single item and add much more weight to it than it merits.

May be a cause of friction, because your companion can feel the need to step around you on eggshells for fear of being offended.

15.   You're Hypersensitive to Criticism

You are always looking for critique. That is why you are so eager to examine any single bit of what your companion is saying or doing. Your self-esteem is so weak that you're convinced that your companion is upset with you. So if there ever be an overt attack, the mind flies into a whirlwind of defensive strategies so aggressive counter-strikes. You really can't do this in the manner people should develop more emotionally matured.

16.   You Have Repressed Anger

While not always the case, there's a fair possibility you'll keep a touch of rage deep inside. This spills into the water sometimes. You might be experiencing outbursts about issues that sound trivial. And you may feel resentful of your mate for no apparent cause. Nonetheless, it's hard to find the root of those emotions. If rage enters into every partnership, the partnership would be brought under pressure.

Throughout these points, it is fuel to add to the fire ignited by some amount of the items.

17.   You're controlling

You are attempting to control your fear, but doing so demands that you still regulate everything else. The breakup issues undoubtedly derive from previous situations when you didn't have an influence on the result.

The implication is you're attempting to micromanage your life and partnership in an effort to escape identical circumstances with the same outcome.

Scared of the unpredictability of letting go and windsurfing. It will lead your spouse to feel inferior as a person because they have little ability to make their own choices.

18.   You Pick Unavailable Partners

You prefer spouses who are either inaccessible at present or completely incompatible with you. It allows you to escape any circumstance that may result in emotional involvement or demand that you engage completely in a partnership. From the past, you might choose somebody you realize was unfaithful. Or somebody's lifestyle doesn't relate to yours. Anyone who is fast to walk on. And maybe somebody that's currently in a separate relationship. You know nothing bad is really going to come out of it, so that is always a relief.

19.   You Sabotage Relationships at Every Opportunity

Some of the issues that we've written of now are manifestations of self-sabotage.

Hate loss and resist not hitting a stage where the way it has been in the past will destroy your heart. You are driving away your spouse, scraping them with snarky remarks, behaving in ways that are not conducive to a romantic partnership. Yet on autopilot, you do it. This is an involuntary method of defense intended to avoid mental distress.

20.   You Blame Yourself for Every Breakup

If you have real problems with the breakup; you are not going to have very strong long-term partnerships. And you can't help but bear all the guilt and liability for the one that comes to an end. You claim you have never been strong enough for themnot mentally, not psychologically, not emotionally. You became persuaded that the stuff that didn't work out as your own.

Are you really having trouble with the abandonment? Here's a simple test: rate yourself from 0-2 on any of the above signs where 0 means it doesn't matter to you, one means it's sort of valid and two means it's precise. Scores of 20 or more indicate a possible structural problem while something above 30 indicates you have a deep resistance to some form of abandonment.

How to Overcome Abandonment Issues

The agony and anxiety that comes with feeling rejected can be traumatic and sometimes stays with us for our lives. Although that's perfectly normal, it implies that we don't really thoroughly pursue every chance we're granted. It's no joy at all to exist in dread and never be 100 percent confident in our circumstances, but there are avenues to push forward.

Here are few ideas for resolving problems of abandonment and you'll live life to the full:

Let Someone In

Big improvements begin with tiny moves. Teach yourself again to trust – this should not be as painful as it seems, don't worry. Confiding in strangers doesn't necessarily involve revealing your deepest, darkest secrets; begin by showing friends the little things they don't learn about your life. Through exchanging knowledge, you can improve your connections and know that people are involved in your life and are invested in it. With time, you will discuss items that are more important to you and do not seem as daunting as they once could have. By easing yourself into the habit of sharing, you can encourage yourself to be more comfortable around others and not always feel too stressed. Trusting others is a major move in every partnership, from anyone of near family members and the guy you are dating and becoming the best mates. If it sounds awkward at first, don't beat yourself up – this is perfectly natural. Travel at a rate that fits you, and allow yourself time to understand that not everyone can undermine your trust.

Find an Outlet

Consider a secure space to share your distress and anxious thoughts. These should not be communicated with others, so write down as notes in a notebook or set up a password-protected site. This helps you to share how you feel, freely without any fear of criticism. Talking down stuff also lets one understand them more easily, which is a helpful way to let it all out. When you're always having trouble communicating about your personal life to strangers, journaling is a wonderful way to continue. Whether it sounds more normal to you to sing or produce works of art, go for it. You don't have to express why you're doing something (unless you want to), just hold things to yourself as an escape. Song-writing is a wonderful means of sharing the emotions, and songs by other artists will also help us understand how we feel. Sports may also be a positive optionthe desire to be part of a squad that needs to contribute to each other. This feeling of belonging and appreciation for one another will act as a nice reminder that you can rely on others.

Own Your Feelings

Part of focusing on your emotional well-being (selfconfidence, relationship problems, and anxiety) is knowing how you feel. Hiding in the warmth of denial can be too simple, and not even acknowledging that something seems frightening or troubling. Although in the short run, that sounds good, in terms of going on in our life, it doesn't do us any favors. Rather than rushing into covering up or suppressing your emotions, continue to focus on identifying them. When it comes to meeting new people or attempting interaction, it's normal to feel insecure or reluctant. Often, we all self-sabotage to stop being completely involved in interactions. We will learn to act in a healthier way, which benefits us by stopping and having an 'evil' thinking or feeling stay in our minds. If a bad thought pops up, don't sweep it aside automatically. Understand what it involves and what it has caused – maybe gazing at old images or talking to a single person. We will start moving on, connecting ourselves with positivity and encouragement through understanding what makes us feel those things.

Try To Rationalize

The desire to be logical is something that may also seem unlikely. You may realize you're totally out of reach, but you still feel helpless to consciously alter your actions. We ought to calm back occasionally to remember what we are really doing. For starters, being preoccupied with somebody leaving us may contribute to clinginess. Looking back to situations that you have behaved in ways that have irritated your spouse may be so helpful.

Leaving seven voicemails when they've been nipping out with some buddies for a drink at the time might sound like a nice idea, but a few weeks in, you'll know this is dangerous. When you think of this action, you would typically feel surprised or a little ashamed. Seek to hold the sensation in your head – not torturing yourself and feeling bad for it, just acting as a warning about what that happens. Remembering your ability to unconsciously overreact will aid in improving your patterns and rerouting how your mind functions.

When you go for the phone next time, think back to how it looked last time you remembered how you were behaving. Leave a note, and set the mobile back down. It may be challenging at first, so modifying so breaking bad patterns would be difficult for you. With time, though, you should be able to sit back and think at stuff before you leap to practice. This will allow you to feel positive about yourself, which will also boost relationships. Your buddy or acquaintance won't sound like they're being checked on all the time, so you won't waste hours (so tons of energy) looking at your screen and trying to send a response through.

Meditate On It

This is in part due to taking the time to weigh the consequences of your actions, but it also relates to being conscious. Mindfulness and reflection are great forms of changing your attitude and being more in tune with your emotions. Such a form of self-work will help one dig into deep-rooted emotions, which are so valuable when it comes to coping with and resolving loss issues.

Such feelings can occur following parental divorces, breakups, death, or general transition of some sort. They leave you concerned that your loved ones are going to die on you – either by option or situations outside their grasp. Although it is to be hoped that such emotions can't govern any part of your life.

Meditation is a wonderful way to resolve and thoroughly express these thoughts of fear. Feeling left in your mind can also feel like the hardest thing on earth, but it isn't as overwhelming as it seems. Practice being alone by sitting comfortably outside, shutting your eyes, and focusing on your breath. It would sound difficult at first, and you definitely won't be able to turn off at all. But, the longer you work, the simpler it can get, and less difficult.

Use this moment as a chance to calm back and to cool down. It's already an accomplishment to move from 5000 thoughts a minute to 3000, but don't be harsh on yourself. Through meditating (maybe utilizing a directed exercise like this) and taking some time to look after yourself, you'll begin to view your actions and emotions differently and eventually giving you more power back.

Assess Your Relationships – All of Them

Often it's not just our overactive thoughts that cause us to think about being discarded-the the individuals around us always affect how we behave. One can make you feel cherished and cared about, and you will still be concerned that they will leave you behind. So many mates, family members, and spouses do you really make yourself look good? Make sure that you are surrounded by loving people, and be as relaxed as your mind requires you to be. Getting into poor habits is too simple and enabling unpleasant people to stay in your life.

It's not a negative thing to let go of stuff that doesn't fit you-it's all right to be greedy when it comes to being rid of toxins. Allow time to evaluate your connections and the individuals you're dating, and make sure they all feed you in every way. There are some people who simply aren't right for you to be with, no matter how much you feel for them. Anyone that makes you feel more anxious, more stressed, or more depressed than usual really won't help you solve these issues. It may be challenging, but if there's still somebody keeping you off, you won't be able to make any change.

The hidden desires that lead to unfaithfulness and their Solutions:

There are several different factors in the marriage that cause someone to become unfaithful.

We're not only learning what makes a happy marriage and family; we're grinding that out for every person one at a time in the trenches every day. We are discussing the deep inner impulses that lead us to slip into unfaithfulness. The goal here is to help you recover, discourage this, or protect the partnership from reoccurring again. Through our field of marital therapy, we dig very deep into the reconciliation partners.

Hidden Desires That Lead To an Affair:

Most individuals are likely to have an affair if they want to feel desirable and respectable. We deserve to learn if there is someone involved in them. People who have these kinds of affairs are typically what we call "Sick Pursuers." They're sick of their partner failing to satisfy their desires, and they've experienced endless disappointment. This changes too far over time, and they lose faith.

Everything arose when the chance introduced itself. We don't necessarily deliberately work out unfaithfulness. Even anyone beautiful pays attention while merely searching for love and innocent relation. The relation is alluring and frustrating. It obviously feels amazing when someone's paying them, love. This sets in rhythm a chain of events that causes the Tired Pursuer to separate himself from their inattentive spouse. The possibility suggests there is a future outside the mediocre partnership to which they have been linked.

The Lack of Trust That Leads To Infidelity; It's Not What You Think

An Avoider's going to get a battle for different purposes. For any point in their life, they avoid trusting others, usually early in their infancy. They can be someone who is very healthy, optimistic, and outgoing, but on the surface level, they remain. They suppress their feelings, which are weak. They are uncomfortable revealing deeper interpersonal circumstances, more open. For them, it is a hostile land. They do not know how to control their feelings because they were never trained.

For example, imagine yourself in a scenario as an avoider, I would claim, "I'm really insecure being near to someone. I find it challenging to trust them entirely. It's challenging to encourage me to depend on someone. I'm anxious when someone comes so personal, and then they expect me to get more involved than I feel confident." I might suggest, "I just don't trust you" while at the same moment, "I'm worried that you're so clocked."

The question is, they do require some. Since we all need others. After all, we are human beings.

How Islands Become Unfaithful Spouses

The avoider turns off their desires and impulses. This is necessary to remember that the feeling they shut off is existing. Both human beings that usually work have these feelings, but some of them have not known how to control them. Those people are known as avoiders. They have been very effective at throwing out and reducing the anger in themselves and in others. Withdrawal avoiders, anytime there's a disagreement, they slow down, they get silent, and they hang off. They simply do not want confrontation. And they are trying to push off such big weak feelings. They develop much animosity over time.

What's At the Root of It All?

Both of the Tired Pursuer and the Island are genuinely terrified at the core.

Islands are unwilling to hand themselves up to another human entirely. It's very tough to completely trust another human. These people have a very weak dedication to a commitment and often. As a way to stay in charge, they hold their commitment level low. They can't let others do them any harm. These people have all the strength. They will abandon you first, by not pledging any of their deepest desires or sharing them.

Tired Pursuers are scared they'll face further disappointment if they keep seeking in their partnership. These people are never going to get their needs fulfilled.

They're scared they're going to start putting all the time forward, and their companion won't respect them. They will try to suppress their interests and ignore their wishes.

They are scared they will never get the friendship they really desire. They are scared they will never get real joy. They're going to keep offering the absolute best to themselves and never receive their spouse's best in exchange, or maybe they'll see the most in what their partner has to give. There's actually not a ton there. They just may not be prepared to do much. These people also believe like in this situation; they would only cut their losses and try joy where joy is feasible. Perhaps they just got married to a dud?

Giving the Best Away

If a Tired Pursuer thinks they're offering the partnership all when their Island partner isn't, finding the Island has been unfaithful is especially complicated.

Some of the first stuff that Tired Pursuer says is, "You're communicating with that guy more than you shared with me." They envisage their stoic, nonemotional, non-intimate partner holding intense, insightful interactions with a stranger and enjoying heated sexual experiences.

They think they are a completely different entity with the participant in the affair than they are with them. The tragedy is that the Island does not really offer something different or unique in the affair except what it has already offered in its union. They obviously had sex, and in months or years, we haven't had that. So, in the end, one will give up being consistently bizarre.

Giving What We Don't Have

Remember that they don't know how to give what exactly you want from them. And they don't send it to the participant in the affair. They can't just be weak, to let someone else in. And they don't actually give more to the partnership than they provided to yours because they don't know-how.

They may have sex with this other individual or whatever, but they don't really have them in their insecure dark places, which is where real intimacy is created.

It can sound personal, as there are letters of affection, roses, videos, sexting, and stuff like that. Yet they really don't offer much else. Suddenly, they don't physically become a separate individual. That is not usually what occurs.

Searching for what Seeds Are Planted Early On That Leads Someone to Infidelity

It begins early in their lives. It starts in infancy.

Part of it starts with parents who are often oblivious and inattentive to their kids. Another part of major things where you expect a family to support you or defend you, but they don't. When the incident is large enough, they will lose their parent's confidence and actually conclude that we need to seek to rely on ourselves. It's when they're an Island. That's why they start slowing down and walking forward. This is when the patterns this contribute to an unhealthy marital partnership begin to develop.

Why Do Pursuers Pick Islands?

The Tired Pursuer begins only like a Pursuer. They are being told at an early age that they have to do it because they want to get their needs met. They need to get noisy; they need to get furious; they need to fight to meet their needs.

We get hurt occasionally. When we get injured Pursuers, tend to be scared of other pursuers, and we get mixed up with the hardcore Islands. Yet the Island feels secure. Yet they can't fulfill the requirements we spoke to earlier over time, and we like we have to try much further. Before we are all burnt out. We are fatigued.

A Pursuer then begins feeling much like an Island. That is when the Island gets scared. Roles continue to turn. The Island is beginning to feel more like a Pursuer, and the dance is shifting.

Why Do Islands Pick Pursuers?

A client questioned, "So if they're only going to keep her out and not commit themselves completely to this partnership, then why do they pick her to start with? What have get them married? Were they bent on being cruel and on ruining her life? "

Above all, they did not want their form of resisting bending. Neither of us wants to be a Pursuer or an Island. It's all offered to us. We learn that from the parents who brought us up. We learn this. Second, at our heart, we all just want the link. We just want to love and be loved, and for that, we are human and made.

The question is that we have learned damaging methods to fulfill our needs. Even in a time when we simply had to shut down to live, we know certain processes. Yet we only go so far as we continue to utilize these bad methods in our romantic relationships. We've got to find different ways to communicate. It may be very frightening as it needs us to lay down the barriers that have supported us in certain areas of our lives. It needs a lot of confidence. Because we've never had anyone we can run to, depend on, and confidence in our lives, hoping that we should get somebody we might feel unlikely with.

What Is The Solution?

The first move to support is understanding what a person wants to have to feel comfortable and lower his walls. And build the environment in which they feel free to do so.

Most of the time, a Pursuer has to explain what they say to their partner on the Island. Yet if the Island partner continues professing a fresh feeling of weakness to a TIRED Pursuer, then the TP typically does not accept it. This will get stronger.

To help manage the sensations of shock, rage, hurt, and the multitude of emotions experienced during the shifts. Help all partners respond in a manner that supports the changes. Instead, the long-term improvements solidify. Nobody wants to waste his time and resources on anything they cannot carry home for the rest of their life, right? You tend to hold to the job you do in matrimonial therapy. Now, bring in motion the necessary stuff to make this happen. There are approaches to having discussions about recovery. Ways of knowing as we slip into our old routines. Ways of shaking off patterns. Ways of changing things yourself around. The better it gets, the more you do it. The first basic step is a determination to improve and an ability to think carefully before trusting others, which will work on.

6.2 Focusing on Transference:

It defines a condition in which one person's emotions, wishes, and perceptions are diverted and transferred to another. Transfer is more generally referred to as a therapy environment, where a therapist can add those feelings or emotions to the therapist.

What Is Transference?

Transference is a concept used by psychology to characterize a process in which an entity redirects emotions and feelings from one individual to another, sometimes unconsciously. This cycle may arise in counseling where a client expresses emotions towards — or perceptions of — another individual to the therapist and then starts to communicate with the therapist as if the therapist is the other party. The trends shown during the transference can also be indicative of a childhood partnership.

The idea of transference was first defined in his 1895 book Studies on Hysteria by psychoanalyst Sigmund Freud, in which he discussed the profound, severe, and sometimes involuntary emotions that often formed inside the therapeutic partnerships he built with those he was treating.

It is a common occurrence among humans and can often occur in therapy, but it does not necessarily imply a condition of mental health. Transference can often arise outside of counseling in different contexts and can shape the foundation for certain forms in partnerships in daily life.

Types of Transference:

More common types of transference include:

●**Paternal transference:**

Paternal transference, when a person sees someone else as a parent or an idealized father figure. The person can be viewed as strong, intelligent, and trustworthy, and an individual can expect the person to offer security and sound advice.

• Maternal transference:

Maternal transference happens when another adult is viewed as a mother or an idealized maternal figure. This individual is also seen as caring and powerful, and they are also required to provide love and comfort.

• Sibling transference:

Sibling transference can occur when there is a lack of parental relationships or when they break down. In addition, this form of transference is not defined by leader/follower behavior, but by peer or teambased relationships, as opposed to parental transference.

• Non-family transference:

Non-family transference can be observed as individuals view the therapist with an idealized image of what they are supposed to be instead of who they actually are. That way, assumptions will shape. Of starters, priests can be assumed to be pure in everything they do, while at all times, policemen can be expected to uphold the law, and physicians can be expected to heal any disease. •

Sexualized transference

Sexualized transference, sometimes classified as either erotic or erotic transference, may occur when a client develops a sexual attraction for his or her therapist.

While erotic transference often refers to an individual's sexual thoughts as unrealistic and can be a positive type of transference, eroticized transference is a consuming attraction toward the therapist, which can be detrimental to the therapeutic relationship and the progress of the client.

Throughout ordinary circumstances, transference is often seen, such as when:

- A person becomes quickly irritated by a classmate who looks a little like their sometimes annoying younger brother.

- A young adult approaches with tenderness a far older female coworker as she brings back memories of that individual's now-deceased mother.

- An entity continues to distrust a new partner solely because a previous spouse has cheated.

Change may be either optimistic or bad. These forms may benefit from various methods of conducting counseling. Positive conversion can cause the individual to see the therapist as caring, interested, or otherwise helpful. Negative transference may allow a client to channel angry or negative feelings against the counselor, but the therapist will also be able to utilize these emotions to help the individual develop a better understanding of them.

Transference in Therapy

Transition can affect a person's social relationships and mental health, as transference may contribute to unhealthy habits of thought and behavior. The primary concern is usually the assumption that an entity does not try to develop a relationship with a real person in the case of transference, but with someone to whom they have projected emotions and feelings.

When transference happens in a clinical environment, a therapist will be able to better interpret a patient through acquiring awareness of the expected emotions and helping the person in the counseling attain success and healing from this new understanding. Through recognizing how the transference happens, a mental health professional may better understand both the state of an individual and/or facets of the early life of the person that influences them in the current.

Throughout counseling, transference may also take place between a psychiatrist, and a client can be termed as counter-transference. The psychiatrist, for example, maybe seen as an all-knowing mentor, a perfect lover, the leader of a person's fate, a formidable foe, and so on. Psychoanalysis proponents agree that transference is a vital psychological resource for interpreting implicit or repressed emotions of a person. Healing is considered more apt to arise if these root problems are identified and resolved effectively.

A psychiatrist may also be able to educate an individual in the therapy to recognize different situations in which transference can occur. Techniques such as journaling may allow a counseling individual to identify possible trends in both thinking and behavior, through analyzing and contrasting past entries. As instances of issue transference are more apparent, a counseling individual will be able to discuss whether the transition happens to hopefully avoid recurrence of the transference.

One form of counseling called transference-focused therapy (TFP) harnesses the transition happening in therapy to help people gain insight into their own patterns of behavior and thinking. Borderline personality disorder (BPD) is most often treated like this.

6.3 Focusing on Projective Identification

Projective identification

Projective identity is an implicit illusion that distinguishes elements of the self or an individual entity and assigns them to an external object.

The projector can sense the projected aspects as either good or bad. Unconsciously intended to induce the receiver of the projection to feel and act in accordance with the projective fantasy may or may not be accompanied by evocative behavior.

Often illusions of projective identification are thought to have 'acquisitive' as well as 'attributive' qualities, implying that the illusion entails not just getting rid of facets of one's own psyche but also accessing the consciousness of the other in order to obtain desirable facets of one's psyche. Projective and introjective fantasies act together in this case.

There is an implicit belief among British Kleinian that 'projection' and 'projective identification' mean the same thing, and that 'projective identification' is a refinement or expansion of Freud's idea of
'projection.'

It can also be defined as:

A defense mechanism in psychoanalysis or psychodynamics in which the individual project's qualities are unacceptable to the self onto another individual, and that person internalizes the projected qualities and believes that they properly and justifiably characterize him or herself.

In Melanie Klein's object relations theory, a defense mechanism in which a person imagines that part of his or her ego is split off and projected into the object to harm or protect the disavowed part, thus enabling the individual to maintain a belief in his or her omnipotent control. One main aspect of Klein's paranoid-schizoid status is projective identification. Building on Klein's work, the British psychoanalyst theorized that in the normal development of communication, an infant would project part of his mind into an object in order to have that part of the mind felt and understood by the object.

Major focus on it:

Projection is the implicit act of attributing someone to something within oneself. The "item" we're projecting is typically but not always an unwelcome emotion or trait. For e.g., if John doesn't feel confident about his own body image, he might see Mark and say to himself, "Hmmm, it looks like Mark's put on a lot of weight." Now, if Mark really put on a lot of weight, John will clearly be correctly examining the fact. Although Mark hasn't added weight, we can confidently presume John is putting on Mark his own supposed unattractiveness. Through projecting into Mark, John is, therefore, distorting his own capacity to objectively interpret truth.

The projection takes place within the mind of one human. In the illustration above, the simulation takes place within John. Mark can walk by John and have no idea what's going on about John's expectations of him.

"Projective identification" is a two-person process. Let's use the above scenario but let's interact this time with John and Mark. Let's presume John meets Mark, welcomes him, and then remarks to him, "You look like you've put on weight." Mark, appropriately enough, can feel insulted, and/or upset, and/or humiliated by this remark. Nonetheless, the origin of Mark's awkward feelings will be carefully scrutinized, as it is at this moment where we have to determine if this duo correctly perceives truth or if they have reached a mutual psychotic condition. If Mark has indeed gained weight, his unhappy feelings that clearly represent his own feelings about the condition of his own body in the aftermath of John's remarks. Since Mark hasn't lost weight lately, we might claim he's been associated with John's perception of painful body image sensations.

Thus, Mark falls away from the sensation of engagement wounded, angry, and humiliated, although he really has nothing to feel injured, upset, or ashamed. He basically gets trapped with awkward thoughts, "keeping the package" that don't really belong to him in the first place.

If Mark hasn't really added weight, we might say he has every reason to feel insulted by John's very disgusting remark, but it wouldn't make sense for him to think about his body appearance, because there's nothing to complain about obviously. Notwithstanding this, it's easy to see how Mark would go home and start staring in the mirror, thinking over how his suits match, or anxiously preparing his next gym workout. If the case plays out in this manner, we might continue to see the risks of agreeing with certain people's projections: basically, we start losing our capacity to accept our own opinions, beliefs, emotions, and feelings. We continue lacking a profound understanding of the contents of our own minds. It refers to the profound value of being willing to trust one's self and building healthy barriers in the face of expectations imposed on us.

And they're fired, from nearly all, all the time. We all project; we all have parts of ourselves that we wish to get rid of, and we all have emotions that are latent, and it's natural that we indulge in this realitybending endeavor. Within our psychological limits, we also still have vulnerabilities, which ensures we are vulnerable to agreeing with other forms of predictions. When this occurs, we join another human into a mutual space of illusion. It is not prudent to continue, for obvious purposes, into life expressing a conviction in lies.

Many significant relationships in people's lives may be based on vision and projective identity in part or in full. The combination of the continually irritated critic with the apparently inept, bumbling companion is one typical partnership that includes this dynamic. Employers and workers, married people and single partners, and parents and children often carry this projective identity structure into their continuing partnerships, much to the annoyance of everyone.

Part of psychotherapy is to start wondering what life would be like, and then what life would feel like if the couple's respective partners could step out of their role in projecting or identifying. What exactly will happen if the manager didn't learn any of this? Or if the consistently inept employee will still excel every now and then? In a family, it is always painful for the consistently "wronged" partner to look at his or her connection to an ongoing issue. In these prolonged dysfunctional partnerships, though, the old adage of having two for tango is still true. Of course, it is not shocking to assume that avoiding the issue in these partnerships requires avoiding the projective cycle, which in effect implies making someone embrace and focus on the distasteful facets of himself or herself that were previously not regarded but merely predicted. Who needs to gaze at the bad bits of oneself?

Hopefully, we all will. It seems that the only way to live a logical and healthy life is to learn to contain our unwanted feelings, not to pass them on to someone else.

6.4 Focusing on Acceptance and Forgiveness

Forgiveness: How to Do It, Embrace Acceptance, and Move On

Trust is tricky-it's difficult to gain and easy to lose.

This is one of the essential cornerstones of any partnership, too. The person being deceived can feel deeply distraught when loosing, and it will totally change the course of the entire relationship. We've all endured some sort of hurt or treachery, but how far? The essence of the friendship, as well as the degree of pain that we experience, is likely to decide whether we are able to forgive the person that deceived us.

It's crucial to note that redemption is a decision, and ultimately the only one that has to deal with the effects of whether or not you chose to be innocent. If it comes to it – keeping a grudge is an enticing and simpler choice, but this action would not be of longterm value to you. The following are a few quick benefits of preferring forgiveness over grudging:

• Reduced stress rates

• Healthy core

• Lower blood pressure

• Improved digestive system

• More sleep

• Fewer distress or thoughts of frustration and depression

• Happier marriages

Forgiveness is simpler said than achieved; even while there are repercussions for keeping grudge, it is not simple to select forgiveness. Until you dive into reconciliation, it is necessary to take the time to analyze and appreciate the case.

So how do you choose forgiveness?

The first step in really deciding that you are willing to forgive or not is to reframe the meaning of it. Most people misinterpret forgiving as "giving in" or condoning the person who deceived you with the actions/words. Some may believe that involves pretending that their acts didn't directly impact you. Forgiveness is NOT to say you were mistaken when you are not. It doesn't mean that you always have to sustain a bad friendship that doesn't benefit you.

Try reframing the concept of forgiving to reflect this:

- Understanding that you are better off after you do so
- Failing to endlessly revisit traumatic events in your mind
- Recognizing that grudges do not help you, but forgiving does
- Saving your resources and committing your attention to something that helps you
- Finding peace with your history.

Until you reframe your meaning of Looking for the lesson in forgiveness, too, is necessary. When reflecting on appreciation, you can find out what you should gain about the case, rather than what you have taken.

What if you can't forgive?

It's a common misinterpretation that if you've been compromised, there are only two options: forgive or bear a grudge in truth that is not the case. Complete acceptance is a third choice that you can prefer lesser-known. Until you are spiritually comfortable, you cannot push yourself to forgive. Acceptance is, in a way, the phase before pardon. In using tolerance, you get to grips with the other person's wrongdoings. Instead of getting vengeance or obsessions with the abuse, you're searching for a motive behind it. Unforgiving tolerance is still a major aspect of going on.

Moving on:

Part of what makes it more important to forgive and understand is that after you have done it, you no longer reflect on what happened. You have made the decision formally not to continue on mulling about, put up, or address the issue. As already stated, one of the advantages of forgiveness/acceptance is going forward and gaining development from the case. This does not imply ignoring what happened to you entirely, just learning about it, and defending yourself in the future. Instead of finding vengeance, strive to live your life by stepping on in the strongest possible way.

Acceptance- the foundation of lasting Relationships:

The bond is essentially chemically regulated when two couples come together first; intimacy runs naturally, and any conflicts or discrepancies are generally missed, misunderstood, or portrayed in a positive way. In time, the simplicity of innocent happiness gives way when we work together, and intimacy wanes, we continue to recognize that closeness causes tension and familiarity contributes to frustration at best and often to absolute disillusionment with the stuff that we see and hear from our companion that we really do not want.

Research shows that there are essentially five ways in which a romantic partner will cope with frustration and disillusionment, each of the different degrees of effectiveness:

1. **Tolerate.** Being put out, but preferring to stand up to the other guy. To accommodate someone is kind of like dealing with a trick knee – you get fits from his or her foibles, so you only recognize a poorer standard of life. It can be frustrating, distracting, or even humiliating, or sometimes unpleasant, as the foibles are.

2.   Retaliate. Retaliation will take one of two forms – leaving the other individual in the lurch and good riddance, or girding one's loins for battle. Like the pair in the film War of the Roses, several partners consider a continued way to communicate across tension while emotions of affection have expired. America's divorce rate is over 50 percent, and we know what a vast percentage of individuals do as they experience disillusionment – sprint for the hills.

3.   Manipulate. Humans are masters at convincing us to do whatever we intend. We're using remorse (Okay, I'm just your mother – the one who struggled to give you life through childbirth), embarrassment

(you annoy me), anxiety (if you don't improve I'll leave) and rage (you haven't seen me mad yet!). We even cajole, criticize, snipe, stonewall, nag, and oh yes, model our partner's 'good' behavior. If the coercion has a favorable or a negative slant, the person being exploited is never satisfying. An attitude of "there's something wrong, repair it," is a tough basis for a partnership.

4.   Negotiate. We get into the purview of psychology now. Therapists enjoy bringing two individuals into a space and meditating, which is a nice way of suggesting that each individual offers a little bit of concession so that either person will declare a victory. There was the bear's account and the hunter who met at a lake where the bear fished for lunch. The hunter put up his hand as the shooter drew a bead on the bear and said, Wait a minute, let's chat. How would you want it to be? The attacker sneered and told him that he likes a bear-coat for him. And the bear wants lunch – maybe if the hunter just put down the rifle, they might come to a resolution, bear added more. Half an hour later, the bear muttered on the grass and burped, "well, he got his coat, and I got my lunch!" Negotiation leads to the answer no as much as it does yes, so two parties never quit the impression that they have received a deal.

5.   Relate. Relating is simply about embracing the other and, above all else, is dedicated to that other, including what we want. Acceptance is accepting the other person for who he or she is, and being moment by moment attentive to the nature of the partnership. Commitment is a situation in which one's marital spouse understands that you truly support him or her, even though differences occur. Commitment does not give space for deceit or disillusionment, only recognition. Acceptance and dedication implies no secret desire to alter one's spouse or to leave. Acceptance and commitment eschew the quid pro quo aspect of a marital partnership between spouses – If you love someone, then he'll love you. Communicating from a place of acceptance and commitment is more like a marriage relationship, a one-way engagement – Someone wants to love you regardless of what you do or don't do for him. It offers a basis for confidence and intimacy between people, which you find in yourself. So it would be like iron sharpening iron while there is stress, two individuals whose working together allows the rough edges to smooth out with time, contributing to maturity.

And how can we switch beyond tolerating, retaliating, manipulating, and negotiating into relating? The secret to this is acceptance. Enjoy your mate regardless of the characteristics and attributes that render each of us special, not in lieu of that. Nobody is flawless, and no two individuals can be completely matched on every question.

Disagreement is expected to occur in marriages and is natural. In reality, the dispute is not inherently detrimental to the partnership in and of itself; work has found that what counts most in connection satisfaction is not how much you encounter tension, but rather the ratio of negative contact to positive interaction. In fact, people that have five good experiences with each one negative experience appear to be happier with their partnership. All of this being said, the settlement of conflicts will be tremendously improved when couples are welcomed by each other.

Needless to add, embracing others seems to be much better than recognizing ourselves. However, we will promote our desire to embrace our spouses by embracing ourselves for certain characteristics and qualities that render each of us special. In others, we also condemn traits that represent hated traits within ourselves. Eventually, practicing selfcompassion will strengthen our relationships with others, particularly with our romantic partners.

Acceptance and Choice as key ingredients for marriage:

Acceptance and choice in the sandbox for a marriage will also create a difference. Acceptance, which is often simple, often not so simple, maybe the toughest difficulty. It could be the first piece of advice a person will get when you get married. Marriage will test your endurance and unconditional lovemaking capacity. Why? For what? Since the guy you get married can see you at your most insecure, and that may be a little awkward to others.

When questioned what the secret to happiness is for people who have been together for several years, the answer has been, usually, we reflect on good qualities towards each other. The initial love process where the dopamine rates are going through the roof subsides, and you take a glance at your companion and start seeing the little stuff that could bother you. You can either stress the small things, or you can try to forget it when it happens. There, choosing is the secret because it's not just one day; it has a good decision every day.

The top seven problems currently, according to the Huffington Post, are constant arguing, where one person needs intimacy, and the other doesn't, alcohol or substance misuse by one parent, a conflict in opinion on work-life balance, financial tension, weight concerns and disputes over adult children.

Many do, but not always dig down to acknowledgment. Try to consider answers where appropriate, instead of sparking claims. Instead of judging or just finding a partnership counselor who will support both of you, focus on the union. Often people want to solve their own issues, but they have to remember that they are not experts in the partnership. Coaches in partnerships will make a difference when you are trying to solve issues that you might be very close to.

Marriage is 80/20 with an individual. They can satisfy 80 percent of your requirements; you only have to find out whether that 20 percent is a necessary need. When you chose to split, note that the law of 80/20 extends even to the next person you want to marry.

Acceptance doesn't give up on oneself but instead use strategies to accept and focus through the complexities of a partnership, like how to tolerate something you can't alter about your mate. More specifically, when it comes to your spouse's biggest concerns, consider with your heart and mind.

Conclusion

The relationship is just like the two wheels of the vehicle, which keep it in balance and help in moving forward without any difficulty. It means that both individuals have equal responsibility towards the relationship. Both should work hand in hand if there comes any hard times in the relationship. To keep the relationship alive, both should have trust and faith in one another. Encouragement and appreciation for one another in a relationship will help the individual to do more for one another. It also gives the individual self-confidence and courage to perform better in life as well as in a relationship. The best way to keep the relationship healthy is to communicate. Communication is the key to every single relationship, whether it is with the family, friends, or your partner. An effective way of communicating is making clear what you want to get from your partner and what you expect from them. It is also important to communicate in a peaceful and calm manner even if the arguments tend to be heated up. Listening attentively and waiting for your turn to talk is also important. One should not interrupt the other while he or she is talking, or it will worsen the situation. Active listening, along with the communication is the best way to resolve the issues. Financial stability and being equally responsible for house chores and outside the house tasks give life to the relationship. Both of them should have respect for one another and their families as well. Relationship is all about give and take. Whatever you invest in your relationship is what you get back.

References

'I Have Relationship Anxiety—Here's How It Affects My Dating Life'. Retrieved from https://www.health.com/relationships/relationshipanxiety

10 Tips To Help Overcome Negativity In Your Relationship - Lessons For Love. Retrieved from https://www.lessonsforlove.com/310-tips-to-helpovercome-negativity-in-your-relationship/

6 Obvious Signs You Are in a Negative Relationship. Retrieved from https://www.marriage.com/advice/relationship/negative-relationship/

6 Toxic Relationship Habits Most People Think Are Normal. Retrieved from https://markmanson.net/toxic-relationship-habits

8 Ways Jealousy Is Good for Your Relationship. Retrieved from https://www.womansday.com/relationships/datingmarriage/advice/a7493/jealousy-is-good-for-you/

Retrieved from https://www.quora.com/Why-isunderstanding-important-in-a-relationship

Could Negativity Be Hurting Your Marriage?. Retrieved from https://www.verywellmind.com/isnegativity-hurting-your-marriage-2300514

How To Deal When You're Arguing With Someone Totally Irrational. Retrieved from https://www.mindbodygreen.com/0-25556/how-todeal-when-youre-arguing-with-someone-totallyirrational.html

Relationship Anxiety: 16 Signs and Tips. Retrieved from https://www.healthline.com/health/relationshipanxiety

Should You be the More Understanding One in the Relationship?. Retrieved from https://theartofcharm.com/art-ofdating/understanding-one-relationship/

Tips for Building a Healthy Relationship. Retrieved from https://www.helpguide.org/articles/relationshipscommunication/relationship-help.htm

When Is Jealousy Irrational? by Monica A. Frank, Ph.D. Retrieved from https://www.excelatlife.com/articles/irrationaljealousy.htm